Kwame Kwei-Armah

Volume 1

A Bitter Herb

Big Nose

Hold On

(Originally titled Blues Brother Soul Sisters)

Introduced by **Andy Hay**

Published by House Of Theresa books

First published in 2001

By House Of Theresa Books
The production house
169 Evering Rd
London N16 7BH

Printed in England by Intype London Ltd

All rights reserved

Copyright Kwame Kwei-Armah

Kwame Kwei-Armah is hereby identified as author
Of this work in accordance with section 77 of the
Copyright, Designs and Patents Act 1988

All rights whatsoever in this work are strictly reserved.
Applications for permission for any use what so ever
Including performance rights must be made in advance, prior
To any such proposed use, to Lou Coulson Agency
37 Berwick Street London W1V 3RF.
Nom performance may be given unless a licence has been obtained.

This book is sold subject to the condition that it shall not,
by way of trade or otherwise, be lent, resold, hired out or otherwise
circulated without the publishers prior consent in any form of
binding or cover other than that in which it is published and without with out a similar condition
including this condition being
imposed on the subsequent purchaser

A CIP record for this book is available
From the British Library

ISBN 0-9541226-0-7

Cover photo Kwame Kwei-Armah as Clovis
in Coventry Belgrade Production of Big Nose
September 1999 Phototgrapher Ian Tilton

CONTENTS

Introduction

Foreword

A Bitter Herb

Big Nose

Hold On

INTRODUCTION

I was aware of Kwame before I met him. He's one of those type of guys. You can't miss him. He's tall, lean, loud, intelligent, good looking, good humoured and black. There's always a kind of turbulence around him, an energy field that seems to either disturb or ignite those other minds and bodies in the near vicinity.

Whilst associate Director of Nottingham Playhouse in 1986 I was visiting Derby Playhouse, a near theatrical neighbour, to see an adaptation of Moll Flanders. Sat in the small hushed bar before the performance I was treated to the first sight, or perhaps I should say the first sound of Kwame as he bounded like a cross between an Afghan hound puppy and a stalking panther through the grim, atmosphereless room. He was laughing deep from his belly, talking at top pitch in a raw London accent spiced with his families Grenadian dialect and standard English. He cut the air with a freshness, a vitality which was at complete odds with the tawdry, conservative surroundings. He had all the confidence and swagger of a young contender. Unafraid and unashamed he almost seemed to dare the institutionalised dominant cultural establishment to challenge him.

The odd thing is, I don't recall his performance in Moll Flanders. What I do remember was an ill fitting costume and a terrible sense that all that enviable, chaotic, visceral force I had witnessed in the bar had somehow been subjugated to it. His soul certainly didn't belong to the merry England of Moll Flanders.

A year or so later we worked together for the first time, at the Octagon Theatre in Bolton where I had become Artistic Director. It was a musical theatre piece with Black American Soul music at its core. Kwame sang like a dream, a young Marvin Gaye and Otis Redding rolled into one. He revealed the star potential he still possesses. He also revealed his growing political consciousness

One day in rehearsals he questioned a line which had as an affirmative reference point "out of the blackness into the light". We spent some time discussing the hidden politics of language, the inherent prejudice in many seemingly innocent everyday metaphors and aphorisms. The company were fidgety, Kwame was fired and I admired him for his passion. He felt the phrase in question reinforced prejudicial and negative attitudes towards 'blackness' and it's direct association with people of African descent. His determined view that we would not change society until the language of domination was eliminated, was not shared by the company or the writer.

The late 80's was a period of stupefying political apathy. I changed the line. Not so much to give Kwame a small victory or doff my cap to PC, but to endorse his growing individual voice in a sea of profound deafness.

During our next production he performed at Bolton, some months later, he played tapes of Malcolm X speeches during the half hour before the performance to the assembled company in the shared dressing room. It wasn't an option! He hadn't asked them, but no one ever objected! The company consisted of both Black and white performers. I use to hear the tape playing from my office directly above. I tried to imagine what the faces of those actors looked like and what was going through their heads. It made me smile. No one took him on. The tapes were part of his studies for an Open University degree.

The Afghan puppy was gone.

In 1995 Kwame came to the Bristol Old Vic where I had moved as Artistic Director. I directed him in a fairly unmemorable show except for one thing-Kwame told me during rehearsals he had a play he wanted to write. I commissioned him.

To live in a society that has no moral external consensus, that is dominated by the culture of narcissism and driven by the imperatives and politics of money making is to be left bereft of bench marks and standards by which we can judge our individual and collective actions. Through out our working relationship Kwame and I have striven to make some sense of the chaos, for ourselves at least. In particular we seem to keep returning to the concept of nationhood and belonging. Kwame possesses a triparteid nationality -African, Caribbean and British. He has the clearest sense of anybody I know of who he is and where he belongs. Here in Britain.

These three plays are a testament to Kwame's enormous capacity for life and learning and his manifest reservoir of tenacity. He has taught me much.

Andy Hay   6th August 2001

FOREWORD

I was sitting in the Siddons bar area of the Bristol Old Vic theatre one pre show evening in February 2001, feeling rather proud of myself. This was not the egotistical kind of proud, which of course we are all prone to, but the kind of pride that comes from the fulfilment of a dream.

The dream was to see my play 'a Bitter Herb' staged. However what my dream had not catered for was the audience reaction. I had missed the first ten performances due to shooting commitments on Casualty, but from that point on I had tried to catch a bit of the show every night until it closed. Nearly every night as the play approached it's end, one could audibly hear the sounds of people either crying, holding back tears or wiping them away. To say that this experience moved me would be an understatement. It touched me beyond words. However let me say without hesitation, that I do not take sole responsibility for the effect the play was having on the audience. An overwhelmingly huge factor was the fantastic performances of the cast, and at that juncture of the play particularly Ellen Thomas who was playing the part of Valerie. The other was of course the meticulous direction of my old friend Andy Hay.

I owe a lot to Andy Hay. It was he that got me into the idea of writing for theatre. It was he that first commissioned me, that then patiently and enthusiastically nurtured my playwriting skills but most importantly it was he that took the risk of staging them. In the economic climate theatre finds itself in at present, this was a brave and honourable thing to do. I pride myself on the fact that the response from the audiences, particularly for '*Herb*' but not forgetting the huge response to '*Blues Brother Soul Sister*' proved his decision to be a correct one.

Anyway back to the Siddons bar. Malcolm Fredrick, the producer, director and in this case actor (He was playing the part of Willard in 'The Bitter Herb' and had wonderfully played the character of Mr Dubois in Chris Monks and I's Big Nose) came up to me and in a tone that that implied 'I'm going to ask you a question and I want you to think about it seriously' said in his wonderful Trinidadian accent " Kwame, have you thought of publishing a collection of your plays?"

"No" I replied, wondering if a publisher was hiding behind his back, because Malcolm is capable of such acts!

"Well you should". And off he went to warm up, which I believe was to put on Willards suit and walk up and down the corridors of the theatre until he was called to stage.

"Thanks I will." I remember shouting back

Well actually I didn't think about it again until *Hold on...* was in rehearsal. Malcolm didn't know that but out of the blue he called me up and said, "Yu tink 'bout dat book yet?" Damn I thought, if ever there was a time to do it was now. My first commercial venture was about to hit the road, and a new series of Casualty was about to begin with my character having a higher profile than previous years. (Well, one and a half actually) So I quickly hustled it up. I found some one to publish it, got Chris to post me the performance draft of the Big Nose script, got Andy to write the introduction and Voila, here it is.

Now unless of course you saw the show I don't expect that one will get too much from reading the text of *HOLD ON*. But if you did then I'm sure it will bring back wonderful memories of Ruby Turners Fantastic performance as Orletta or the charm and pomposity of the Rufus Collins Character she spent most of the show fighting. However in the preceding two pieces, *A BITTER HERB* and *BIG NOSE*, I do hope that the ideas and themes that I have tried to explore will have some resonance with you.

In 'Big nose' the joy was to tell in part, the story of my parents and their pioneer generation set against the huge backdrop of unrequited love. In Herb it was to highlight some of the mistakes made by the country that invited them and the all pervasive philosophy of assimilation that seemed to engulf those same pioneers and effect that had on the lives and minds of their children.

So to commemorate the launch of the *Hold On....* tour, here it is, my first three plays in the order that I wrote them.

Kwame Kwei-Armah   August 3rd 2001

Kwame Kwei-Armah is Writer in residence at the Bristol Old Vic Theatre and Associate writer at the Tricycle Theatre London. He is currently working on commissions for Royal National Theatre Studio, and a new contemporary Gospel Musical for the West End.

Dedicated to my Mother for always believing

Thank you God, Bishop Brown my spiritual advisor, Andy Hay for having faith, patience and standing for something in an age where few do, my brother Paul for exactly the same, Sister Ann Marie, Fyna for looking after the children often single handily, my father for always being there. Michelle for love, Malcolm Fredrick for the inspiration behind this book, Chris Monks for 'the joy of the Nose', Bob Eaton, my Children Kwame, Oni and Kofi, and again my mother Theresa for creating the family infrastructure that allows me to be a father, a son and an jobbing artist. You will forever be my role model.

Bitter Herb was first premiered at the Bristol Old Vic Theatre Feb 2nd 2001. The cast were as follows:

Valerie McKenna	Ellen Thomas
Willard McKenna	Malcolm Fredrick
Jaime McKenna	Amelia Lowell
Peter McKenna	Mark Theodore
Naveen Patel	Shan Khan

Directed by Andy Hay
Lighting designed by Tim Streader
Designed by Penny Fit

Bitter Herb was awarded The Peggy Ramsey Bursary 1998

Characters

Valerie The matriarch. She is a West Indian Woman in her early fifties. Having done very well for herself in business, her accent swings from RP to West Indian when she's angry or upset. It would seem that she does not like Black people very much

Willard Her husband. A laid back Fifty something.

Jaime Their White daughter. 22 yr. old.

Peter Their youngest son. A shy 21 yr. old

Naveen Law coalitions head man. He represents the family

SCENE ONE

*The stage is empty. We are in the front room of the comfortable home of the McKenna family. A middle class black suburban household. The furniture is more heals than Ikea. We hear a car pull up in the drive and the sounds of a person getting out and closing the door. A key turns and the front door opens, but we do not here it close. There is a big picture hanging on the wall of a young man at his graduation. On either side of it are two smaller pictures of him. One of him laughing the other of him as a three year old. We will later discover that the young man is **John**, the eldest son of the family.*

*Enter **Valerie**, looking very elegant in her funeral blacks. She is in her fifties but looks younger. She is the major breadwinner in the family and is pleased that every one knows it. Unlike Willard who has more or less retained his native accent, much to Valerie's annoyance, Valerie is a very well spoken west Indian woman. Her native accent only really coming out when she is angry. Valerie owns and runs three nursing homes for the elderly. Employing nearly a hundred people, and Willard, after receiving redundancy from British rail, helps her to run them.*

Just as Valerie steps into the room the phone rings. She rushes to answer it

Valerie   McKenna residence, oh Yvonne....... Fine thank you, how are things at the home? Good... The vicar gave a very moving speech and you know, he's in the ground now. What can you say! Is everything all right with Mrs. Anderson? Her drugs? Good. Ok I'll be back in tomorrow morning... listen I must go. Thank you very much, I'll pass it on to the rest of the family.

While Valerie is on the phone she sees a fax that arrived while they were out. She collects it and reads. She tuts aloud.

VALERIE   Oh for heavens sake, I can't deal with this now.

While she is reading the lights suddenly dim. The pictures of John on the wall are the only things that are illuminated. It is like that for a few beats before Valerie calmly and playfully says

VALERIE   Jaime stop playing the fool and put the lights back on.

*Enter **Jaime**, the families white adopted sister. She is in her early twenties, in fact there is only a year between Peter and her, and is the personal officer for the business.*

> *On the whole she is a very happy go lucky kind of girl. Although race has never been an issue in the home, she sees herself as a woman who is Caribbean. She does not play or attempt to impersonate black street cultural habits, but due to her life long environment has a deep understanding of West Indian culture.*

JAIME   How did you know it was me?

VALERIE   (*She smiles*) Who else does stupidness like that? You really are your fathers child.

JAIME   Oh but when you want to show me off I'm your child eh?

VALERIE   (*Jesting*) Who'd ever want to show off an ugly child like you

JAIME   Funny I'm always told that I look like my mother!

VALERIE   Your mother may be ugly but she shrubs up nice.

> *Jaime runs up and hugs her*

JAIME   You're the most beautiful woman in the world and I adore you. Still think your bottom looks a bit in that dress though

VALERIE   Does it?

JAIME   Only kidding. You left the front door open?

VALERIE   Did I darling? I knew you were close behind.

JAIME   I take it the boys haven't arrived yet?

VALERIE   No. But they should be here Then again you who knows with those two. I'm just going to check on the food.

> *She runs up to the photo of John kisses her hand and then places it on his face*

JAIME   Love you bra. Thank you for making it a nice day. It was a nice day wasn't it? I mean you could have disrupted it and that. (*Playfully*) Your angry spirit could have come and mash up the place. But you didn't. I felt peace. Thank you John

> *Valerie enters the room while she is taking to John. She watches her for a bit.*

VALERIE	You are such a loving child huh Jamie.
JAIME	All your children are
VALERIE	(*Purposely correcting her*) Were.

BEAT

VALERIE	You know what really vexes me about this thing, it's that those thugs didn't just take away our John, they are slowly eating away at my family. Look at Peter, anger is eating away at him. I am his mother, I should be able to find a way to help him through this
JAIME	But you're angry mum!
VALERIE	Well yes of course I am. But I'm angry at the injustice of it, Peters angry at the world. When it's that wide you can't focus. Has he talked to you?
JAIME	He hardly speaks to me. Maybe Dad should ….
VALERIE	(*Kisses her teeth*) Who? Your father?
JAIME	Once they've been caught he'll settle down. He's a big softy you know that mum
VALERIE	Yes but will he be our big teddy bear anymore?
JAIME	No. He is a big man now.
VALERIE	Eh, never mind how big your children get, they're still your babies. Remember that.
JAIME	For what? I'm not having any
VALERIE	So you don't want to make me a grandmother?
JAIME	Oh yeah sorry I forgot. I'll just pop down to the local sperm bank on the way home from work tomorrow
VALERIE	If I was young enough, the moment John died I would have another child. Bam. Just like that. I thought about it, hard. Just five years younger. As I laid in that bed howling like a wounded beast, I kept trying to find reasons to get back up. You know what on the seventh day got me out of that bed?

JAIME (*Tongue in cheek*) The hand of God?

VALERIE Don't mock the Lord child

JAIME Sorry

VALERIE Someone whispered in my ear, I don't know who, "Get up. Whose going to be strong for the children you have left?" And you know the next day I got up out of my bed, and have never cried since.

Jaime knows because it was her but she listens.

VALERIE And I know people were looking at me today thinking 'what a hard woman I don't even see a tear come from she eye' but I know what was going on in my heart.

JAIME I knew that you were being strong for us mum

VALERIE Good

We hear another car pull up.

VALERIE Right, lets fix up before the men arrive. Should never let them see you weak.

Jaime hugs her mother. Then as if shaking off the grief returns to her former self. They go into a routine that they are familiar with.

VALERIE Who are the rightful rulers of the earth?

JAIME Women folk

VALERIE Who do you go to when you want a proper job done?

JAIME Women folk

JAIME And who are called birds because they pick up worms?

VALERIE Women folk

BOTH That's right.

*Enter **Willard**. The father of the family in his funeral blacks. He is in his mid fifties. Even though he is a quiet man by nature, he has sadness about him that is very tangible.*

WILLARD   All you still doing that stupidness?

JAIME   Hi dad.

           She runs up to him and gives him a kiss

WILLARD   I hope you doesn't do that to every man you know

JAIME   (Playing him) Just you daddy

WILLARD   You mouth to damn sweet

JAIME   Well who I learn from? (She takes his jacket)

WILLARD   Thank you darling.

           He walks up to the photo of John, looks at it for a second and then enters the room

           Valerie holds up the fax

VALERIE   Willard, the builders needed a decision before midday about the disabled entrance at Elm house. Isn't this your responsibility? Why are they sending the fax for my attention?

WILLARD   I'll call Harold tomorrow

VALERIE   That was midday today

WILLARD   I'll call them tomorrow Valerie

           Valerie cuts her eye at him and picks up the phone

VALERIE   Hello, can I speak to Mr Thompson please? Hi, Harold! This is Valerie McKenna, McKenna nursing homes. I'm so sorry we've not got back to you but look, could you bear with us until close of play tomorrow? We would be ever so grateful! Thank you so much. OK Goodbye.

           She cuts her eye at Willard again.

VALERIE   In business, a little courtesy goes a long way

*Enter their twenty one year old youngest son **Peter**. Peter is shy and forgiving by nature, however now is developing into your classic angry young man. We can see he is in a bad mood. He puts on the TV and sits on the sofa*

WILLARD Peter you lock the car door properly boy?

PETER Yes.

WILLARD Yes who?

PETER Yes Dad

Willard and Valerie clock each other. Jaime tries to be playful with Peter but he does not respond

JAIME (*Impersonating dad*) Eh eh you losing you manners. You must want me to cut you arse!

VALERIE Who are you speaking to in that vulgar manner?

JAIME Can you believe that Michael Andrews asked me out at the graveside.

WILLARD Who?

JAIME Michael Andrews, Auntie Julie's eldest

VALERIE Well, that family's hardly known for their subtlety. I mean look how Julie was dressed. Breasts were all hanging out of that thing. I was praying that she didn't come to the edge of the grave, they'd have pulled her in I swear.

Jaime giggles

VALERIE But wait, doesn't that boy Michael drive for some courier company or something?

JAIME I think so?

VALERIE What would make him think that my university educated daughter would have any thing to do with a manual worker?

JAIME Mum!

VALERIE   West Indians! They will always amaze me! Tell me why we must make a spectacle of ourselves at every occasion? I saw some people breaking down and damn right bawling today that hadn't seen John since he was about five years old

From the kitchen

PETER   At least they showed some emotion

VALERIE   Jaime now that the boys are here could you help me get the food out

She gets up and heads for the kitchen

JAIME   But Peter's right there!

VALERIE   (*Kisses her lips*) What does he know about food and kitchen, hurry up girl before the food boil down for true

WILLARD   I don't like that timer thing all you does use

VALERIE   Huh, it was different when John was here eh, I didn't have to go near the stove. Every night a different cordon bleu meal

PETER   It wasn't every night!

VALERIE   He'd come home and experiment on his next dish, follow it with the most superb desert. Huh

She exhales. Silence

VALERIE   Those were the days huh. (*As if talking to John*) Hmm John my child, they got me right back in front of the stove.

JAIME   You know I dreamt John last night. He was smiling all over his face.

WILLARD   That's good. It means he's happy. And after six months in a fridge, time the boy body thaw out in the earth.

Valerie changes the subject slightly. She will not tell anyone but she is upset that John has not revealed himself to her yet in a dream

VALERIE   Peter don't just stand there. Get the wine from the fridge. And it's White

Peter kisses his teeth. Valerie stares at him while the rest of the family gently look up.

PETER — What?

VALERIE — Something wrong with your teeth child?

He leaves for the kitchen with much attitude. Valerie picks up a card from the neighbours

VALERIE — This is such a beautiful card. Listen to this. "Some people are sent here for a short time, but the light they leave behind will shine forever" We miss you John. Isn't that lovely?

JAIME — Who is that from?

VALERIE — The Goulds next door.

PETER — Considering they hardly spoke to John in his life, I'd say it was closer to amazing.

VALERIE — I don't know what you have against those people.

JAIME — They think were freaks.

VALERIE — What are you talking about freaks? The only thing freaky about this house is that I have, had three West Indian men in here and not one of them is on state benefit!

JAIME — Mum you are so out of order.

VALERIE — You're talking to me about freaks and I'm telling you what is freaky about this family. I despair for some of the younger generation I really do

PETER — And why's that?

VALERIE — Because they're lost. The Government gives them all this social security for nothing, it's taken away they're desire to work. I'm sorry to say but too many young people today are under-educated and work shy

JAIME — That is not true mum

VALERIE — Yes, it is. Alright look at that girl Sawera, Sabina

JAIME   Saniqua

VALERIE   Saniqua or what ever her name is at Elmhurst home, that girl is work shy, the same for Joan at Dane house, and Eric at Pivot house, these people do not like to work. But mention the word party, oh my god.

JAIME   We are very hard working, those are only three people...

VALERIE   Those are three West Indians that we employ, or should I say that you employed. I asked Eric the other day, no I said to Eric "Did you go to see your mother this weekend' and do you know what he said, 'No Mrs Mac, I didn't went. I mean, a boy born and bred in this country answers 'I didn't went!'

JAIME   He didn't

VALERIE   I promise you he did.

JAIME   No he didn't went I saw him on Sunday (*Laughs*)

VALERIE   Stop it.

             Willard smiles

VALERIE   Tell me who other than my liberal minded daughter is going to employ some one who cannot even speak his native tongue.

PETER   Mum did you ever stop to think that they might be creating their own language?

VALERIE   That's ridiculous. Own language! They should learn to speak English first

JAIME   Mum you are so reactionary

WILLARD   (Half speaking to himself but pointing at Valerie) You'd never think it was English boys that killed our John would you?

             Peter looks over to the TV. Peter calls his mother very nonchalantly.

PETER   Hey it's on. I knew it was Network South East cameras

Willard looks up at the TV and then gets up and leaves the room. Valerie comes out of the kitchen area and sits on the sofa next to Peter

VALERIE   Unmute the thing na!

TVNEWRDR   .... was buried today in his home town of Southham. Tension between the local community and police have risen significantly over the last six months, due to what the some believe to be a racially motivated attack. We spoke to a person close to the McKenna family

VALERIE   Who is that?
(*She looks to Peter*)
Oh my God it's one of your Black Nation cronies.

PETER   What you looking at me for?

NAT'MAN   Justice is a fallacy for many people in my community. The killing of John McKenna, another innocent Black youth is testament to the fact that we live in a nation where the Black life is valued less that that of his fellow white countrymen. Where are the perpetrators of this hideous crime? Still out there on the streets posing a real threat to decent families. The question we have to ask ourselves is, is this because of police apathy or police conspiracy

VALERIE   My god, people like that infuriate me. Take it off, switch it off.

JAIME   Well at least it made the local news. That's more than we've since John died

Peter switches it off.

VALERIE   Don't they realise that they are only making it worse for us. Every second it's race this and race that. John was killed. All I'm interested in is finding and punishing the killers. That's it.

PETER   It's not as simple as that mummy

VALERIE   Not for you and your cronies obviously, you want to wrap it up with all of your political nonsense. I spoke to the police liaison officer only yesterday and he assured me that they are doing all they can to gather enough evidence to successfully charge the boys

PETER   How long have they been saying that?

VALERIE	Rome wasn't built in a day. I'm telling you Peter, you and I are going to fall out over this Black Nation thing.
PETER	Why are you taking out your rage on me? I didn't talk to the TV people
VALERIE	Yes, but it's you that has bought those people you associate with into our family business. What you children don't realise is that the English do not respond to all this noise you want to create. Quiet dignity, that's what impresses them. The sooner you learn that the better.
PETER	So they respect a woman whose child has been killed yet she remains silent?
VALERIE	Relying on the proper authorities to do the job they are paid to do is not remaining silent
JAIME	(*She shouts*) Dad dinner
	Willard enters the room, sits down at the table. As does Valerie and Peter. Willard senses that something has been said. So tries to soften the atmosphere.
WILLARD	Ah fish broth. A good choice Valerie.
VALERIE	Well it was the boys favourite. The dumplings aren't as fine as John made them ….
WILLARD	….And you is the West Indian, shame on you. Huh, that boy made dumpling like my mother. And he was an Englishman you know.
PETER	(*slight edge*)That's because you taught him dad.
WILLARD	No because he was interested!
JAIME	Mum, aren't you going to say grace?
VALERIE	(A thoughtful pause) Let your father
WILLARD	For what we are about to receive may the lord make us truly thankful amen.
VALERIE	(half whispers) Is that it?

Willard opens his eyes and looks at Valerie. She does not return the look but instead coughs to encourage him to finish the prayer. He closes his eyes again and continues

WILLARD And em, thank you father for allowing the family to share this meal together. I thank you for my family. Amen.

JAIME Amen

VALERIE Amen. Let's help our selves shall we.

PETER Kushangilia, Tamshi La Tambiko

Valerie shoots Peter a dirty look.

VALERIE What nonsense are you saying child?

PETER It's African, to be exact it's kwaswahili for ancestors thank you for being with us, and …

VALERIE (*She gets a little West Indian*) Don't tell me anything about no African business

He stares at her with contempt.

PETER Mother we are….

VALERIE Better still don't bring that inside this house. You understand?

PETER I understand mother, the question is do you? You know what If you'll excuse me I'll have my dinner in my room.

VALERIE You'll do no such thing.

She looks to Willard for support. He looks at Valerie and then to Peter. He attempts a compromise that will give Peter a little space but will get him back to the table

WILLARD Peter, go and put me tie in my room and then come back make we eat as a family na?

Peter nods and exits. Valerie calms down. The others are looking at her.

VALERIE Willard you really must take responsibility and deal with that child. I don't know how much more I can take of this, believe me.

WILLARD I go talk to the boy.

VALERIE Talk? I've been talking till I'm blue in the face, talk is not enough. This Nation business is sending him crazy. It's them that make him drop out of university you know that don't you?

WILLARD (*To Jaime*) My grandfather use to say there's no place like your parent's house, I remember...

VALERIE Oh darling let's not have another of your grandfather stories, really.

JAIME Ignore her Dad, I like your Grenada stories

VALERIE Ah! Go on then.

He was going to anyway

WILLARD Well I was simply reminded of the fact that my grandfather never lived with my grandmother. They had a house together had several children but every morning before the sun would rise he would be back in his mothers house.

JAIME Why?

WILLARD I don't know, apparently his father did it and every time I asked him why he'd simply say 'there's no place like your parent house boy'.

VALERIE (*Valerie cuts in*) Go on you've missed out the best bit. He use to always say 'boy I like all kind of tea, bush tea, china tea, every tea except

Jaime and Valerie finish the sentence

FAMILY responsibilit- tea'.

Willard chuckles to himself. The others smile

WILLARD Yes granddad, responsibility, can be a bitter herb

VALERIE It's that kind of lazy attitude about responsibility that has kept us West Indians down.

There is a knock on the front door. Jaime jumps up

VALERIE Willard get the door will you.

JAIME   It's all right dad, I'll get it.

Peter enters the room. She quickly moves towards the door

WILLARD   Thank you Jaime. You see, when I leave every thing in my will to that girl people go say she's me favourite. But see how that girl always look out for she father?

*Jaime opens the front door. She sees **Naveen**, a smartly dressed Asian man in his mid thirties. He is from the law coalition.*

We hear off stage.

JAIME   Can I help you?

NAVEEN   I am so sorry to disturb you. My name is Naveen Patel I'm from the.. May I come in, I'll only take a minute of your families time must speak to your family urgently, it's about John

JAIME   What about John?

NAVEEN   I think I can help

Jaime pauses for a while and then lets him in.
She leads him into the front room. We see that he has a card in his hand and a newspaper.

JAIME   Mum dad, there's gentleman at the door says that he has…

WILLARD   Yes we heard

NAVEEN   Good evening my name is Naveen Patel and I'm a partner at South East Law Coalition. First of all may I extend my deepest condolences and my profoundest apologises for disturbing you on a day like this but, I couldn't stop myself. I had to come over and talk to you.

He hands them the condolence card

VALERIE   Thank you. How can we help you Mr Patel

NAVEEN   I'm here because I'd like to offer my services and that of the Law coalition to your family.

VALERIE   Thank you Mr. Patel, but we already have legal representation.

NAVEEN   Yes I know that, but with respect, I think now, you'll need more than that. You'll need people that have real punch and clout with the media

VALERIE Why would we need that?

NAVEEN   Well because in light of today's events, if you do not your case will simply disappear. If we were to represent you for no fee what so ever, we would not allow this tragedy to be sweep under the carpet

Valerie and Willard look at each other.

WILLARD Why would you do all of this for no fee?

NAVEEN   Because we believe in Justice.

VALERIE Mr Patel, thank you for your offer but at this time I can't see a reason why we would need further representation. The Police are doing their job, why would we need lawyers?

NAVEEN   You have read this evenings papers haven't you?

VALERIE No, I can't say that I have?

NAVEEN   Oh.

WILLARD Why?

NAVEEN   Page 12

PETER   What does it say?

He hands Valerie the newspaper

NAVEEN   The police released a statement today stating that they have taken the case as far as they could with the three youths suspected of Johns murder. That in fact now they're enquiries have lead them to believe that John could have been involved in a gangland drug feud not a racially motivated attack

FAMILY   What? I can't believe that let me see. My son

PETER   What?! It wasn't about drugs

VALERIE ...Drugs?

NAVEEN	It's been on the local television news all evening
WILLARD	No.
PETER	I suppose that's what they meant when they said they are doing all they can eh mum?

This piece of news hits Valerie particularly hard. She hands the paper to Willard and sits down to compose herself. However now she is more interested

NAVEEN	I'm so sorry.

The family are stunned

NAVEEN	Mr and Mrs McKenna I know this has come as a shock to you but let me assure you that this is not unusual.
JAIME	Really?
NAVEEN	In my experience if after six months a murder has not been solved or as in this case, the evidence against the suspects is deemed insufficient to secure a successful prosecution, the file is marked 'Enquires complete' N.F.A. No further action. That file is then put away. It is not a coincidence that on the day of your sons burial that this kind of statement is released to the press. They are burying him too. What I am saying is that I live in this area. I cannot stand by and allow your sons character to be systematically assassinated and the three suspects released because they do not have the proper resource or inclination to solve this case.
WILLARD	Em look, please don't think that I'm being rude but what experience do you and your coalition have in cases like these?
NAVEEN	We looked after the James Wood case last year....
VALERIE	Really, I remember that.

Valerie and Willard look at each other

WILLARD	We are in the middle of our dinner Mr. Patel
NAVEEN	Please excuse me, I'll leave you to it. (He hands his card to Jaime)

He turns to leave

WILLARD Would you care to join us?

He stops

NAVEEN Thank you.

WILLARD Peter set another place at the table. Jaime get the plate please. It would give us more time to hear your thoughts. It's only a simple meal but it was our son's favourite

They leave to do that.

VALERIE So Mr. Patel, tell us about yourself?

NAVEEN I live but five roads away. My parents are from India, and we moved from Glasgow to Southall, West London when I was young. I've been with the coalition for about the last five years. Before that I worked for a solicitors firm in the temple.

VALERIE Right. And this Law Coalition deals with?...

NAVEEN ...Humanitarian concerns

VALERIE Why would you leave a prestigious firm in the temple to do that?

NAVEEN I feel you should put a little back.

PETER Is that it?

NAVEEN Yes. What else is there?

PETER I don't know, you tell me?

NAVEEN When I was about fourteen my father came home from work and whisked us to the top of our street. He pointed to what we knew was a N. F. pub, in an area that was 98% Asian, and said "look son's, justice. It was being burnt to the ground. Suddenly a van filled with the later disbanded Special Police Group, crashed on to the pavement. Out jumped hundreds of policemen who just started throwing their batons at people. We ran. Luckily, we got into the house and I ran straight upstairs to look at the proceedings from out of the window. You know what I saw? Behind the front two lines of policemen were tattoo wearing skin heads with batons and shields. The police had armed them! Does that answer your question?

PETER   It'll do. For now

WILLARD   Please let we eat

They do

Naveen looks to Valerie. She has become very still and silent. It is as if the memory of the night of her son's death has suddenly revisited her.

JAIME   Are you alright mum?

VALERIE   Yes. I simply thought of John while I was listening to the story. So what are you proposing Mr Patel

NAVEEN   What in my opinion you need to do immediately, this is with or without us, you must immediately refute the allegations of Johns alleged drug connections in the loudest possible way. If not the case is dead. Myself, OK I would set up a press conference straight away

JAIME   We don't know anything about the media?

NAVEEN   In cases like these, what you need to know is that they are a necessary evil. Speak to them in the language they understand, they'll come running. You need to grab the country's attention. Get decent law abiding people to pressure the authorities to bring justice to your home. Smearing your sons name to validate inaction well...But it will be their downfall. If there is one thing you can say about this country we have a keen sense of fairness. Now the key issue here is justice but as much as we would not want to use race, John was killed in what appears to be an unprovoked racist attack. The point for me is not whether the attackers were Black or White, it is that they are still at large. The question you need answered is why?

VALERIE   Must we bring up the race thing?

PETER   Of course we should...

Peter is just about to pile in when Naveen indicates that he is better poised to deal with it.

NAVEEN   Regrettably I think so. It is a major factor. Had it been the other way around I doubt if we'd be sitting here having this discussion.

JAIME   (*With a slight attitude*) Don't you think the public are fed up with hearing Black people moan about being Black?

NAVEEN   I agree. But on the James Wood case it was nigh impossible to get the media to give us any meaningful coverage. What Johns case needs in this world of Satellite, cable and digital media is something that will capture the publics attention. And you have it

VALERIE   Really

NAVEEN   Yes you have it in Jaime

He pauses for a second. Peter laughs.

PETER   Ha. Very good. Very good.

Jamie is stunned

JAIME   Wait a minute, If this is a skin tone thing I need to tell you that we don't see that in this family.

VALERIE   That's right, I've haven't raised my children to concern themselves with that.

NAVEEN   Forgive me. But this is not about you or the way you see the world. It is about the way the world sees you. They will listen to you Jaime more than any other member of this family. It's a horrible fact but it's true. If you want public pressure to bear down on the authorities then we need to grab their ears. You simply have the loudest voice.

JAIME   What about Peter, my brother died in his arms. He looked in the faces of the killers

NAVEEN   You have to look at it with the media's eyes. You want something from them.

PETER   They kill my brother and now we're trying to find the best way to get their sympathy???!!!!

Silence

WILLARD   And this is your plan?

NAVEEN Mr and Mrs McKenna , let me be straight with you. If Jaime were to be the family's spokesperson, I could near enough guarantee that with in two months your sons case will be in the minds of every person who cares about justice in this country. I will work for you, if you let me, which ever direction you choose to go in. But I believe in success and I, we at the coalition believe that success lays in our ability to stir the publics sense of injustice. But we have to grab to them first

WILLARD And what if this doesn't succeed?

NAVEEN Then we'll find another way. Let me assure you, we are not prepared to accept the taking of your sons life and the defiling of his family name, lying down. We would do what ever is necessary to bring this matter to the courts.

The family acknowledge his commitment in silence.

VALERIE I see. Do you have children Mr Patel?

NAVEEN I have an 18 months old daughter

VALERIE Huh. Thank you for talking to us.

NAVEEN You can contact me for what ever on the numbers on the card

VALERIE Thank you. Peter see Mr Patel to the door.

NAVEEN Mr and Mrs McKenna, Jaime.

WILLARD Bye Naveen

Peter sees him out. We hear the front door close. Valerie grabs the phone. Peter is in militant mood

VALERIE I need to speak with somebody about this.

WILLARD Who you calling?

VALERIE Our liaison officer

PETER So, what's your view on this mother?

VALERIE (*Losing it a bit*) Peter give me a chance. Answerphone. Inspector Williams this is Valerie McKenna. I wonder if you could call me

	back as soon as you pick this message up. It is a matter of great urgency. Thank you
PETER	So mum what is your view? Should we follow the advice of the Mr Patels law coalition or there is an alternative you've thought of?
VALERIE	I said Peter give me a chance. (*Looking at the paper*) Drugs?
PETER	Mum it's not quantum physics were dealing with here. A/ we go along with this Naveen guy and fight for John or B/ we don't and Johns known forever as a drug dealer
VALERIE	It's not as Black and white as that Peter. I don't know if their strategy is one I would like to go along with.
PETER	You mean you don't know if you want Jaime to feel uncomfortable.
VALERIE	I don't know if it is right that Jaime should be used in this way.
PETER	Used?
JAIME	Yes used.
PETER	How would you be being used?
JAIME	He said it!
PETER	Said what?
JAIME	He said because they see me as…
PETER	See you? (*Beat*) I know we've never acknowledged this before but you are not a light skinned Black woman (He says it with a certain amount of venom) You are white. Why are we deceiving ourselves? Jaime is one of them, let's use that to our advantage.
JAIME	How dare you talk to me like that?
VALERIE	Stop it Peter.
PETER	Stop what? Stop the truth? My brother died in my arms, my arms. If having Jaime do the talking will help to put those bastards behind bars,….
JAIME	(*overlapping*) If Jaime what?

PETER ...then what is the problem? It doesn't stop you loving her

WILLARD Watch your mouth boy

PETER I'm sorry Dad, but is it just me or are we more interested in protecting Jaime than the memory of my brother?

JAIME He was my brother too?

PETER Oh yeah?

VALERIE Stop behaving as if you are the only one whose lost John. He was all of our flesh and blood

PETER (*Screams*) Then act like it.

JAIME What is that suppose to mean?

PETER Read between the lines.

JAIME Oh I get it. I'm not blood now. I'm your sister Peter

PETER You may be my sister but you are not my blood, get it.

WILLARD (*Screams*) Stop this, stop this now.

PETER Why? This is the first time we've had an honest conversation about this. We have lived all our lives denying and hiding and avoiding what is before our very eyes.... and that was cool...

WILLARD I said stop it Peter

PETER But now they are calling my brother a drug dealer and we are debating the only proper offer of assistance we have had. Why? Because we don't want to face the facts that Jaime is what she is?

WILLARD I said stop it Peter

He cools down

WILLARD We are family. Do you understand what that means? It means it's us against the world. Now I for one would rather do nothing than do anything that will harm us. We are all we have. Now I suggest we leave this subject and tomorrow we will decide on the right course of action. Goodnight Peter, goodnight Jaime. Goodnight

They at first do not move. Then realising that they are being dismissed like children they both leave the room.

He sits next to Valerie. She looks well shaken by the argument. Willard is distracted

VALERIE Why would they do that?

WILLARD Do what?

VALERIE Drugs!

WILLARD Why do they do anything?

Willard wanders off. He ends up next to the mirror. Willard pauses.

WILLARD You know Valerie, I look into the mirror and see these grey hairs and say 'but what is this, I'm still a child, I'm not no middle age man'. And then it hits me that I am and that my child is dead, twenty-five and he's dead. And what have I done about it? I have waited and relied on the people that now call my son a drug dealer

Valerie simply looks at him. Jaime enters with her coat on.

JAIME Mum, dad....

WILLARD I thought I told you to go to bed? (*Playfully*)

VALERIE Are you ok love?

JAIME Yes

VALERIE Are you sure?

JAIME Yes I am mum

VALERIE Ignore your brother

JAIME Which one?

Beat

VALERIE Peter was being very silly

JAIME The night after John died someone came up to me and said "It must be so horrible for you knowing that the killers were.." and

	they substituted the word 'English' for white, as we do. So I came home and waited for us as a family to have the discussion about how we were going to deal with that. Tonight we had it
WILLARD	Tonight was not a discussion Jaime
JAIME	Do you remember the time John came home from school, we were about eight and five, and he asked you mum why 'he were so dark and I so light', and did that mean that he was wickeder than I was. Auntie Pearl who was at the house at the time said to him 'no, but if you are good, when you grow up you will have children that look like Jaime'. And then she turned to me and said and you madam are Lena Horne's shade, and no one questioned where she belonged. That was the last time I remember talking about it. I need a little air. I'll see you later
VALERIE	Please be careful out there.
JAIME	I will. (*beat*) You know I will do anything for John don't you Mum?
VALERIE	Yes I know

She leaves.

WILLARD	Maybe we didn't do this thing right you know Val.
VALERIE	How'd you mean?
WILLARD	The boys come out so English and Jaime... Maybe we were wrong not growing her up to be proud of, well you know what I mean
VALERIE	Proud? How were we going to tell her about being..... English?
WILLARD	You know about being English than the English they self Mrs McKenna
VALERIE	What we have had in this family is what they out there can only talk about. How could we have been wrong?
WILLARD	My head hurting me. I think I'll go and run a bath.
VALERIE	OK Let me know when the bath is run.
WILLARD	Why you going to join me?

VALERIE   (*Kisses her teeth*) I'm going to do the washing up. You can't run two
               hot waters at the same time

WILLARD   Right.

               Willard leaves the room looking at picture of John.

                              SCENE TWO

               *McKenna's front room. Peter is sat on the sofa reading. Willard
               walks into the room. He stops looks at Peter and searches for
               something to say to him. Willard has been ordered to talk to Peter
               about his black nation connections, so is looking for a smooth way
               in. Peter is momentarily surprised by his fathers interest.*

WILLARD   What you reading son?

PETER   Oh hi dad. Em, seminal writings on Slavery and the English
               mercantile system by Michael Jones

WILLARD   A little light read I see! (*Tongue in cheek*)

PETER   Actually it's fascinating. Do you know that when slavery was
               abolished in (he looks in the book) 1833, we were given the names
               of our slave masters. Isn't that weird, we carry the names of the
               people that once owned us.

WILLARD   Really! (*Not really interested in that subject*)

PETER   Yes but listen to this, it just hit me when I was reading last night.
               Why have we set up a memorial plaque for John, is it not to
               remember him, to make sure that his name is never forgotten, that's
               right isn't it?

WILLARD   Yes it is.

PETER   (*Thinking it through*) Well then, us carrying the names of our former
               slave masters allow their memories, their names to live forever!
               Can that be right?

WILLARD   People don't study things like that any more Peter.

PETER   Of course we don't, but we should. I remember a time in school
               when the teacher was going through all of the children's surnames
               in the class and telling them what it meant. Tony Baker probably
               meant his forebears baked, or was from a baking area. Etc. etc.
               and when she came to me, she said McKenna, well you're surely

not from a Scottish clan are you Peter. And the whole class burst out laughing at me. I found it half way funny too. Me with a Scottish name. How stupid. But I never stopped to think why, until now.

Willard takes the book from Peter.

WILLARD You know I use to play cricket with Michael Jones back home

PETER Really?

WILLARD Yes, he was a bigger boy to me back then, but I joined the cricket club young. They use to call me Little L.B.; Lightening Balls

PETER Lightening Balls?

WILLARD Yes because my ball would just flash down the pitch.

PETER Yer.

WILLARD And a few other things. Um huh. Michael had just returned from University in England. He could have been a first class cricketer if he didn't want to be in this politics thing

PETER Really?

WILLARD St. George's CC. Boy we were the best in the Island. You know two boys from our team got selected for the West Indies. Tour of 84 me and you uncle went to The Oval to see them play and Curtley Roberts shouted from the slips, "eh eh, look who in the stand na, not L.B". (*He laughs*)

PETER What the Curtley Roberts?

WILLARD Yes. We went out for a drink after the game, boy we laugh about the old days.

PETER Dad you've never spoken about that before?

WILLARD When you get to a certain stage in life you get so bored with you own stories boy, you stop telling them.

He stops for a second remembering John

Your brother knew. He asked me one day if I had any broken dreams. First class cricketer I said. I think I could have been a first class cricketer.

PETER   Why didn't you do it then?

Willard pauses and looks at Peter. He decides to carry on.

WILLARD   What you can't hide from God you can't hide from man. I made a local girl pregnant. It wasn't any old local girl. It was the daughter of a chief selector for the West Indian team. He was also our team coach.

Pause

PETER   What happened to the child?

WILLARD   Oh she didn't have it, but everybody knew she was pregnant for me and, a powerful man in a small island is, powerful. It got so bad that eventually I couldn't get any kind of work. So my Grandfather gave me his life's savings and sent me to England.

PETER   Your granddad gave you the money?

WILLARD   He was a great man you know. Simple, but yet he said things then that I would have to wait thirty years to fully understand.

PETER   Did he ever talk to you of his family, you know his father, grandfather?

WILLARD   A little, I think. He would always say the McKenna's had strong blood. His grand father died at seventy nine, his father died at eighty-four and he'd probably kick in at ninety, just so in heaven he could bust style on them.

PETER   His grandfather must have been a slave then?

WILLARD   (*Mood changes*) I don't know. Old people never spoke about those things.

PETER   But he must have been cos if they abolished slavery in....

WILLARD   Peter let me tell you something, all this slavery talk; it's not good. That was the past, looking back to that can't help anybody, you understand?

PETER   No dad, I don't understand. I don't understand how we can forget that!

WILLARD   Because we have to, it doesn't take you anywhere.

PETER   Do you think a Jew would say that about their holocaust?

WILLARD   (*Momentarily losing his temper*) I'm not concerned about what a Jew may or may not do, but I am about the hate in my own sons heart.

Peter picks up his book and starts to read again.

WILLARD   I know you loved your brother, but he wouldn't have wanted you to hate, and I can see that in you Peter, we all can, especially Jaime

PETER   He'd have wanted me to fight though.

WILLARD   Fight? What is the backside you young people have to fight?

PETER   (*In near disgust*) You see that's what I'm talking about, how can you say what is there to fight? We are in a warzone dad, and we've already had one casualty at the hands of the very people we moved close to to escape own.

WILLARD   Listen, all that Black nation things that you're reading, don't you realise that it is hate their preaching. Hate destroys you from with in son

PETER   (*Loses his temper*) Dad I don't understand you. At least they stand for something. What do you stand for? You know at first I blamed mum for John's death. But now, I blame you. You for not standing up to her like a man when she wanted to move us into this area, when she wanted to make us be so comfortable around these people that we would not see their danger. Why didn't you stand up to her when she wanted to assimilate us dad, why didn't you do something when we became more uncomfortable among our own than with the enemy.

WILLARD   Enemy! Peter what are you saying?

PETER   You know why John died? Not because some racist jumped him, but because you were not man enough to warn us about the evil inside of them. Your complacency father, contrived to make us an easy target. You killed him dad, so don't tell me there's nothing to hate.

WILLARD   What did you want me to do say "No Valerie, I want my kids to stay here and grow up in this stinking council estate"? I did what I thought was best for my children. You make choices in life Peter. And once you've made them, a real man sticks with them. You want something to hate? Well hate me for that.

PETER   (*Sarcastically*) Oh do you want a medal or round of applause

WILLARD   You can be rude, but life is long. I hope you'll be able to say what I've just said when you're my age

PETER   When I'm your age I won't be like you I can tell you. I'd have stood for something my children could be proud of.

He walks out of the room

At that point Valerie and Naveen enter the house. They are a little joyous. They had a little too much wine at the celebratory lunch they just attended. However they are nowhere near drunk.

NAVEEN   And it's because of you Valerie honestly. Ah Willard. Did you see us in today's Telegraph? 'WHITE SISTER CALLS FOR REOPENING OF MCKENNA CASE. Page four. The Telegraph is not one of our usual allies. For them to feature this is a big breakthrough for us.

There is no reply. Willard is still thinking about Peters outburst

VALERIE   Willard, did you hear what just Naveen said?

WILLARD   (*Snaps back*) Em, yes. Well done.

VALERIE   Well done! Is that all you can say?

WILLARD   You two look a little sweet.

VALERIE   We had a celebratory lunch at the office.

WILLARD   I see.

Willard responds with a little smile

VALERIE   So what!? People can't let off a little steam?

Willard does not reply. She kisses her teeth

VALERIE	Anyway what are you doing here? One of us needs to be at Elm house at all times. You know what that family are like. (To Naveen)

Willard gets up and heads out

WILLARD	There are about ten messages by the phone for you.

He leaves

VALERIE	Thank you. One of our more difficult patients fell and the family is threatening to sue. Sit down.
NAVEEN	Is it serious?
VALERIE	Maybe, maybe not. We've been threatened before. Once they've seen that we are taking them seriously, they'll calm down. Anyway carry on with what you were saying.

Valerie picks up the messages pad and reads while talking to Naveen

NAVEEN	Oh yes, I was saying that you are the rock that this family is built upon. I wish I had half your courage. And stamina, my god I couldn't keep up with you at the meeting this afternoon
VALERIE	When you have a hundred old people and their children running after you day and night, you learn to move pretty quickly.
NAVEEN	That's good because now that that we've positively engaged the press things will be moving very quickly. We'll be keeping a constant vigil outside of Scotland Yard and if they don't budge, we'll move to outside of the houses of Parliament.
VALERIE	Will they allow that?
NAVEEN	Yes, it's our constitutional right.
VALERIE	Really?
NAVEEN	After twenty years of paying taxes in this country the rights and mechanisms of the world famous British democracy are there for you to use.

VALERIE   I understand that but Naveen it's the ethnicity bandwagon thing. I have difficulty with. I have avoided it all of my life. I never hide, but I distance myself. That is how you survive in this country.

NAVEEN   (*He thinks*) How many times a week would you say you think about what it's like to live life with a severe disability?

VALERIE   Hardly ever

NAVEEN   Me too. Yet when we meet say a person in a wheel chair we automatically start to talk to them about wheel chair access into restaurants and access to cabs and all sorts of thing. But in that conversation they will tell you one thing about their everyday life that you could not have thought of. And it will stay with you

VALERIE   So you're saying being like us is a disability?

NAVEEN   No. I'm saying this thing is about exposure. If we want the quality of our lives, our children's lives to improve we must be visible we must challenge their negative perceptions at each possible opportunity.

VALERIE   But I have challenged them Naveen. What I do for a living, the way I've raised my children.....

NAVEEN   ....It's not enough Valerie. A reporter asked Denzel Washington what it was like being a rich famous actor and he replied "well I still can't get a taxi in New York after dark".

VALERIE   (*Laughs acknowledging the truth of the statement*)
            That's just people being ignorant Naveen.

NAVEEN   Or is it us that are being ignorant believing that we can truly live in a colour blind world?

VALERIE   Sorry?

NAVEEN   To ask people intellectually to ignore what is physically before their eyes is dangerous. It has huge political and mental implications. And when it is decided that we do see it again what then become of those that bought into that?

VALERIE   So what do you say about Jaime and us?

NAVEEN   The truth or a polite reply?

VALERIE   The truth

NAVEEN — I think in denying or ignoring her "difference", although done for the absolute most honourable of reasons, you have run the risk of creating problems for her in adulthood.

VALERIE — So you're telling me to see my Jaime as different? She's just my daughter Naveen.

NAVEEN — With respect, I know when you enter the big bad world out there, you are very conscious of what she is. You have to be in order to protect her.

VALERIE — This is very uncomfortable Naveen. Of all my children my little girl child is the one most like me

This line of argument has seriously challenged Valerie, in only a way that Naveen can.

NAVEEN — I tell you where all of this has come from Valerie. I'm a little worried. BBC radio called to ask us if Jaime would appear on a new talk show called Britain today. One of the other panellists will be Peter Wright from the BNP. Apart from being evil incarnate, he's very bright. He'll come prepared to well, hit at Jaime.

VALERIE — Then we'll just say no

NAVEEN — Yes we could, but a senior official from the home office will be on the show and it will be our best chance yet of connecting with the only people that really count

VALERIE — I see

NAVEEN — What ever the outcome of the programme, the campaign will benefit, but if Peter Wright turns the heat on Jaime, she could come out very bruised. In a way it would be better for us if she did, because public sympathy and outrage would come to bear in front of the home office. I suppose what I'm saying is that maybe the time is approaching when you and Jaime have a direct discussion.

VALERIE — A discussion about what Naveen? Jaime is a together child. Trust me.

NAVEEN — At one of our media briefing sessions she told me a story once. She said that when she was younger she would get into the bath and scrub as hard as she could. You'd told your children that we all have seven layers of skin, but if you were good and clean, you'd get to the one you wanted most one day. So she kept scrubbing, and being good, but it never came. That is the discussion I am talking about

VALERIE Do you know what it's like the first time you hear your innocent child mention skin colour? It terrible Naveen. Because up until then you've lived in hope that maybe things have changed, that this new generation have lost the curse of race. But when you hear them say, " mummy the white man over there" you know it is the end of the ride. From this point on they will either be oppressed by it or use it to oppress. Well I had both in my house and I was determined that neither would do either. If Jaime's problem is that she doesn't know what side she is on well it's because I wanted all my children to see that there was only the human family. So don't you worry she'll put the family first.

NAVEEN Will you be around when I speak to her about the program?

VALERIE Of course I will.

NAVEEN Good. We're making a difference Valerie.

VALERIE Well I can't have them saying that my son was a drug dealer. And I will take this to the top if I have to

The phone rings. Peter walks into the room. He is on his way out. Valerie turns the collar on his coat down as she picks up the phone. He heads towards the kitchen. While Valerie is on the phone Peter eyes Naveen up. We see that it makes Naveen feel slightly uncomfortable.

VALERIE Hello aunt Marge ....Was she really?..... Good... she's a bright girl... thanks for letting us know. (*Excited*) Naveen, that was a friend who just heard Jaime's interview on the radio, said she sounded great.

NAVEEN Good.

We hear the front door key turn. Enter Jaime. When Peter sees that it is Jaime he leaves the room quickly but with much attitude.

JAIME Hi yer.

VALERIE Hello Darling, I've just put down the phone from Auntie Marge. She called to say she'd heard you on the radio.

JAIME	Really!
VALERIE	She said you were excellent
JAIME	Good

Naveen nervously decides to grab this opportunity

NAVEEN	And We've got some great news. The BBC have called and asked if you could appear on Britain Today with the Home secretary…And a few others.
JAIME	Right. Guys I'm a little tired would you mind if I had my tea upstairs?
VALERIE	They're isn't anything ready. I can russell you up a quick tuna something?
JAIME	Don't worry I'll eat later.
VALERIE	O.K. How was your day?
JAIME	Rubbish
VALERIE	How were the people you interviewed for the Elm house vacancy? Find anyone decent?
JAIME	It was more like they were interviewing me. Every single one of them went on for half an hour about how they felt so sorry for us and our injustice blar blar blar
NAVEEN	That's good. It means we're getting through to the people on the street.
JAIME	It means that I can't properly assess people because they're so busy emoting over me
VALERIE	Don't worry dear. It's all for John.
JAIME	Yes, that's what I keep telling myself.
NAVEEN	I know you've had a long day but can I run a few things by you about this BBC interview.
JAIME	Go ahead Naveen!

NAVEEN   I've said it to Valerie and I'll say it to you. We need this one. It's as simple as that. But one of the other panellist is Peter Wright...

JAIME   Peter Wri? The guy from the BNP?

NAVEEN   That's right.

JAIME   Isn't he the one that said he could not condemn the stabbing of that mixed couple because they themselves were committing racial genocide

NAVEEN   I'm afraid it is

JAIME   (*Outraged*) I'm not going on any programme with him. The man is a monster.

NAVEEN   I know he is but...

JAIME   (*Calmly and coolly*) But nothing, Naveen I wont do it. God can you imagine what he's going to have to say about me.

VALERIE   What can he say about you?

NAVEEN   I know that Jaime that's why...

JAIME   ...You're trying to soft soap me

NAVEEN   Support you.

JAIME   Oh Naveen, come on, as much as I hate it, I do all the radio, tv and demo's that you ask, but how do you justify this one?

NAVEEN   Jaime this one programme will reach more important people than a thousand demo's and local radio interviews combined.

JAIME   Mum we need to talk, would you excuse us Naveen.

He realises he is being asked to leave

NAVEEN   Of course. I'll call you later Valerie

She nods. He leaves. Valerie sits next to Jaime

JAIME   Mum this is ridiculous. I am finding this really hard.

VALERIE	I know it must be a strain. Coming home from work then shooting off to some interview or other, but I am so proud of you. We wouldn't be where we are today with out you. I know it's hard but ultimately it will be worthwhile
JAIME	Will it?
	Valerie decides to broach the sensitive subject
VALERIE	Jaime, have you ever felt, would you describe yourself as different from ……
	Jaime doesn't like where she thinks this is heading.
JAIME	What are you asking me Mum?
VALERIE	Oh nothing. Nothing. Forget it.
JAIME	You mean different from you?
VALERIE	Well….
JAIME	Or different from John and Peter….?
VALERIE	…Well
JAIME	(*with attitude*) well of course I was adopted
VALERIE	I don't mean that, come on
JAIME	Oh you mean as in, racially different?
VALERIE	Like I said let's forget it shall we.
	For a moment she is in a stunned silence.
JAIME	Ha. Wow. Ok. When it was Peter that was one thing. When people in the street started pointing at me that was another, but now my mother is telling that I am different?
VALERIE	Jaime that's not what I meant
JAIME	Well what did you mean Mother when you asked me if I felt different?
VALERIE	I was simply enquiring…..

JAIME	Enquiring were you? Well how come you've never enquired about that before?
VALERIE	Because.....
JAIME	...Because you've never had a son killed by people that look like your daughter is that right? Or am I not that as well now?
VALERIE	Jaime calm down.
JAIME	No I suppose I'm not. I will not bloody calm down. I'm going to these meetings right and people are shouting and screaming about the wickedness of White people and then they ask me to stand up.... I don't know whether they are going to cheer me or stone me. How secure do you think that makes me feel? All the Black people I know don't see colour and then suddenly I'm exposed to that level of rage. I'm frightened to look at any one in the eye in case suddenly they realise that I'm white too and I get lynched. Then I come to the place I'm suppose to have peace and my own mother wants to debate my difference! (*Screams*) I know I'm different all right I don't need you to remind me. Look at this leaflet. Some one shoved this in my face.

She pulls out a leaflet out of her bag

JAIME	Read it. Go on read it mother of mine.

Valerie looks at it quickly and then looks away

JAIME	Tell me what it says then. What you can't read?
VALERIE	(*She reads it*) How long are we going to let these white devils kill our children in the street? What are we going to do?
JAIME	Is that what I am to you mum, now that I'm different?

Offended by the question Valerie doesn't answer. Taking that to mean that she can't Jaime picks up her coat and storms out

VALERIE	Jaime. Where are you going? Jaime......Jaime

END OF ACT ONE.

ACT TWO

SCENE ONE

THREE MONTHS LATER.

> *Lights up. The only thing lit is Willard sat on the sofa. His eyes are closed and he is mumbling to himself. We disappear into his mind*

WILLARD John child? I know we didn't really see eye to eye in your last days, but.. (*Suddenly changing theme*) Tell you one thing that I have learnt, never let an argument fester. Boy I don't know what I could have said that would have bridged our schism, but I wished I'd have tried. It is one thing to lose your first son, to never be able to regain his respect. John I'm not a praying man as you know, but if you are in a place that is closer to God than I am, ask him to give me the wisdom to find a way to heal this family. Jaime and her mother, Peter and his hate, me and my... lies. I don't ask for your forgiveness but help me find the strength to keep this family together. I know that you are listening child, I just know.

> *Lights snap up. Valerie walks with a pile of posters. She rests them on the table.*

VALERIE Mumbling to yourself again Willard?

WILLARD To John actually. How long have you been here?

VALERIE You talk more to that boy now, than you did in the last year of his life. I've just got in.

WILLARD You could well be right. What are these for?

VALERIE Tonight's rally in Welling. I hope your going to be at this one, your absence was very conspicuous at last weeks. Naveen had to make up all kind of excuses for you. People are coming from all over the country to demonstrate for your son.

WILLARD To tell you the truth Val, I don't really feel comfortable around those political types, I don't know what they want me to say.

VALERIE They don't want you say anything, just be yourself.

WILLARD And to be really honest I don't even feel comfortable around Naveen

VALERIE I'll not have you say a bad word about Naveen. If it wasn't for him we'd all be sitting around the front room moping and soaping

WILLARD   Really. Your vicar must have seen you on TV last night. He's called about five times.

VALERIE   What did you tell him?

WILLARD   That you've been avoiding him and the church for the last six months and you'd prefer it if they stopped calling.

VALERIE   As you've never said more than three words to him I doubt if you'd have delivered that sermon. What did you really say?

WILLARD   That you would be back in late. He said they were in the area tonight and wanted to come and share a little fellowship with you.

VALERIE   I see. (*She kisses her lips meaning subject closed*)

WILLARD   I went to see your daughter in she new place today you know

VALERIE   Who? (*Deliberately provocative*)

WILLARD   Jaime!

VALERIE   Really?

WILLARD   Yes really? I think you two are being very silly Valerie

VALERIE   Did you read that letter she wrote to me? Did you hear the wicked, ungrateful and vile things she said about me? Me the one that loved and raised her she's going to call 'the dirty bitch that caused her confusion'.

WILLARD   She didn't call you a dirty bitch

VALERIE   She may as well have, she called me everything else. These ungrateful people

WILLARD   So she's people now?

Valerie doesn't answer him.

WILLARD   Valerie write back to the child please

VALERIE   Who me? Huh. Is she that move out of the house you know, she that leave the family business, that leave me to struggle on for John by myself. She must think that me and she is companion, writing abusive letters and expecting me to reply? She should know me better than that Willard. Any way as Naveen always says, the struggle is a great distiller. When your back is against the wall you'll know where a persons loyalty falls.

For Valerie the subject is closed

WILLARD   Huh! (Changing the subject himself) I'm toying with the idea of going to Grenada when all this is over, what do you think?

VALERIE   How long for?

WILLARD   For good.

Valerie stops what she is doing

VALERIE   For good? What have you got back home Willard?

WILLARD   I don't know, we could sell one of the nursing homes and build a house or little a something!

VALERIE   And what would you do for money?

WILLARD   I don't know, I haven't thought about details. We're not too old; maybe we could start a little business or something?

VALERIE   I'm not going home Willard, there is nothing there for me.

WILLARD   What is here for you Val except heartache and bills?

VALERIE   You think you don't have bills in the West Indies?

WILLARD   But we'd be among our own people.

VALERIE   Willard you think it's easy home?

WILLARD   It's not any harder than here, and at least you wake up with the sun shining

VALERIE   And mosquito's biting, congari, centerpea, you forget all of that?

WILLARD   No, it's just easier to deal with than hypocritical smiles and two faceness. The police, the political people who really don't give a damn about my son. I am tired of these people Val. It's as simple as that.

VALERIE   You think that I'm not? Every time I have to clean one of those old peoples shitty backside, you think I don't remember that one of their children, killed my child? Do you think that every Saturday when I am standing in the cold holding some placard begging for their mercy, that I don't remember that they taught their children the hate that killed mine? Not a day goes pass with out me remembering my son and what they have done. But what you want to do is run Willard, and I've never ran away from anything in my life, and I'm not going to start now.

Willard gets a little irritated

WILLARD   Look at these letters, I've not shown you because you have so much on your plate. 'Leave good White folk alone', 'Your nigger arse is as good as dead, ha,' 'how does it feel to have a dead nigger son.' I don't have to live like this.

VALERIE   (*Changing subject*) I hear your woman is going home next month? Is that what this is about?

WILLARD   I'm sorry?

Valerie looks at him. Enter Peter, who even though he hasn't really spoken to Valerie and Willard properly in the last few weeks, is so excited that he's bubbling over with the need to tell them of his new discovery.

PETER   Mum dad, the best thing happened today, you would never believe it, it was like, oh my god.

VALERIE   (*Offish*) What?

Valerie kisses her teeth and walks off.

Willard knew she knew but she had never mentioned it before. He tries to pay attention to what Peter is saying but for a little while is more concerned with Valerie.

PETER   I haven't told you but I have been going down to the Colonial records office at Kew, where they keep all the historic papers regarding the Caribbean

WILLARD   You haven't told us very much at all lately

Willard retaining a little of the tension they had after Peters last outburst at him. He has forgiven him he has not forgotten

PETER   I know, I know, but look I have to tell you this. With the information that you gave me dad about your family and I went there and asked for Grenada's yearbooks. I'd roughly worked out that my great great grandfather must have been around when they abolished slavery so I ask for the book of 1833,4,5. The woman behind the desk asked me what I wanted it for, so I told her that I was trying to trace my family tree. "Were they Slaves" She asked, "if so you're wasting your time, as they never kept records of slaves or about slaves". Just give me 1833 and shut up.

Willard raises his eyebrow as if to say I know you didn't say it like that.

WILLARD   Boy is you ever going to get to the point?

PETER   I'm getting there wait a minute. So she gives me this book right and it's huge. I mean three hours later I'm still on January. To cut a long story short...

WILLARD   Thank you

PETER   Four forty five arrives and I'm still in April. Woman over the speakers asks everyone to finish reading and return the books. I'm so vex that I just flip over the pages and it lands on September 5th 1833. And what's on that page, swear to god. My great great great great grandfathers name, George McKenna

WILLARD   What?

Suddenly interested

PETER   I swear. I couldn't believe it. There before my eyes. Dad I just screamed. And every one in the office started to applaud, cos they all knew that I must of found what I was looking for. Can you believe it?

WILLARD   What was he doing there?

PETER   Well as it happens your Gt.x4 grandfather's brother was given his freedom when he was really young, and inherited his White fathers plantation. However he was a bit of a dodgy character and was selling bootleg rum to the neighbouring island, which at that time was owned by the French so it was a treasonable offence. To cut a long story short he was caught and the biggest trail of 1833 was his.

WILLARD   So how did his brothers name get into the book?

PETER   They listed all of his family members, but his brother in particular because Alexander McKenna, bought his own brother but only gave him partial freedom, I know it's amazing isn't it? Anyway that's as far as I got today. They had to drag me out of there.

WILLARD   You know what's funny about that, my grandfather always said his father never touched a drop of rum in his life. Said it was the source of all evil. What's more he said that we were suppose to be rich, he never explained why we weren't, but every now and then when things were really hard, he'd keep saying to himself, 'boy we suppose to be rich'

PETER   Wait, your grandfather told you that? That was Angus McKenna right?.

WILLARD   Angey and his father was called Joseph. One big he funeral he had.

PETER   Dad this is fascinating stuff, I might even go to Grenada and check this stuff out properly. I photocopied loads of stuff, so I've got a lot of reading to do. I should have known I was onto something, I dreamt of John last night.

Valerie clocks this as she enters with pieces of wood to stick onto the placards she bought in earlier.

WILLARD   Hurry up, I'm looking forward to hearing about we family

He leaves the room.

VALERIE   I don't know why you are encouraging that boy in all that African Business.

WILLARD   I am not, the boy is interested in the family, I think that is most commendable.

VALERIE   It's probably some project that Black Nation leader has given him.

WILLARD   You confuse me sometimes you know Val. One minute you, you talk of the contempt you have for these people and the next you slam your son for finding out about his family.

VALERIE	You're only interested because it's your family, if it was my side he was looking into, it would be looking back to that slavery thing.
WILLARD	I am not going to go into a your family my family thing.

The doorbell rings.

VALERIE	Get that for me please, it's probably Jack come to collect some of the banners, God I've only done two, it's you and your stupid sons fault. Oh no, if it's any one from the church, I'm not in. I've gone away for a month or something.

Willard gets up to open the door.

WILLARD	By the way, she's not going home.
VALERIE	Is that so!

Willard leaves to open the door. It's Naveen. He rushes into the front room.

NAVEEN	Valerie Valerie, have you seen it?
VALERIE	Seen what?
NAVEEN	This evenings Standard
VALERIE	No Why?
NAVEEN	We are on the road, if Willard weren't here I'd kiss you.
WILLARD	Feel free
NAVEEN	Yesterdays cabinet reshuffle. The new home secretary, he's ordered the reopening of the case, and I quote " Deputy commissioner Jackson has assured me that no stone will be left unturned in the pursuit of justice for the McKenna family"

Valerie and Willard jump into the air and scream with delight. They both hug Naveen.

VALERIE	I can't believe it, I can't believe it.
WILLARD	Oh my God, John did you hear that? Peter!

NAVEEN I was driving home from the office and by chance I saw the headline. I told you that we were on course for victory. We are going to nail them.

Peter hearing all of the noise runs into the room

PETER What's happened?

VALERIE The home secretary has reopened the case.

WILLARD It is great news!

PETER Ha! Masser says he's going to look into the problem so lets have a party. When has he ever done what he's promised? Do you think they are ever going to prosecute three of their own for doing what they have been doing for centuries? It's another nigger out of the way. So excuse me if I don't get out the banjo and bite into my watermelon

NAVEEN Personally, I think that is a very negative attitude Peter. We don't have many occasions to celebrate, I think, if I may say that it's really very churlish of you to destroy this one

PETER Do you now?

NAVEEN Yes I do. Your mother and I, and of course the rest of the family have worked very hard to get even this far.

PETER I must tell you Naveen, I don't trust or like you, please do not lecture me

VALERIE Peter that is enough

NAVEEN No Valerie let him get it off his chest

PETER Don't patronise me either, I have nothing on my chest I simply told you how I felt.

Valerie looks to Willard to say something

NAVEEN Personally I'm getting rather tired with your angry young man act. I think you need to grow up.

Peter loses it and charges at Naveen

PETER Don't you talk to me like that you bloody Asian. Are you crazy?

Willard jumps in the way and holds Peter who is about to hit Naveen

WILLARD Peter what do you think you are doing?

VALERIE Oh my god Peter stop it!

Peter screams at Naveen

PETER No I'm not having him talk to me that way. What are you getting out of this eh, Mr. Humanitarian of the year. I know you people. When there was government money about you guys were Black, now it's gone your Asian again. I see right through you, you money grabber

NAVEEN I have not charged your mother a single penny for this case.

PETER Yer yer yer. You're getting paid, think I don't know that you're getting paid. Who they going to run to every time for a sound bite?

Valerie flips

VALERIE Peter, you're going to swear and talk to people like that inside my house? It's quicker you leave, before I'll tolerate behaviour like this. Apologise to Naveen for this outlandish behaviour

NAVEEN Really Valerie, he doesn't need to apologise.

PETER You would put me out of my home for him?

VALERIE I didn't say leave the house I said quicker...

PETER It's the same thing

VALERIE I am not debating this with you. I said apologise.

PETER I meant everything I said, an apology would be hypocritical, If that means you want me to leave then I will

VALERIE Peter I said apologise, Don't test me child, apologise

PETER (*Half to himself*) I don't need to be here I'll tell you that

VALERIE You don't need to what?

WILLARD   Stop this now. I can see were this is going to end up.

VALERIE   Don't undermine me like this Willard

WILLARD   I won't stand by and see our family furthered destroyed Valerie. He's the last child we have. Let them work this thing out themselves

VALERIE   That's why they are as they are. What a weak father you are. The child will swear up in here like any old junk yard dog and you will condone it? Naveen come. The air in here is too rank.

She leaves the room. Naveen slowly follows her. Willard falls into the chair. Peter looks at this tested man

PETER   I don't know what came over me dad, I'm sorry.

WILLARD   So am I. (*Pause*) I don't understand the point in fighting for your dead family, and destroying your living one! Do you?

SCENE TWO
The lights come up to see an empty front room. The house is not looking as tidy as it normally does. In fact it's looking quite ragged. Valerie enters with her coat on. She is about to go out. But is not looking her usual tidy self. She notices a fax in the machine. She takes it out and starts to read it. She picks up the phone and makes a call.

VALERIE   The small business section.. Gerald Peterson please...Valerie. McKenna of McKenna nursing homes....Hello Gerald, So sorry I haven't returned your calls, yes I've received your fax. .. Um Yes I realise we are pushing the boundaries of our overdraft... no we haven't achieved those targets but I fully expect with in the next few weeks we'd have replaced the patients that we have lost... how do you perceive we restructure? Turn the overdraft into a loan using the equity in our home as security? Right......let me have a little think about that before you send the surveyor round.. I'll get back to you in the morning... I know you are on our side. I just that it's the only thing we have that's our own and one would be loathed to.. Yes I'll speak with you tomorrow.

She puts the phone down.

Damn.

Willard comes out of the kitchen area. Valerie jumps back in shock

VALERIE	You frightened me, I didn't know you were home.
WILLARD	I'm not, I'm on my way out!
VALERIE	As usual
WILLARD	Did you see today's paper?
VALERIE	No? I haven't had time
WILLARD	Read it.

He passes the paper to Valerie

VALERIE	The crown prosecution service announced that it is to review its case against the three youths accused..... A spokesperson for the C.P.S. said that the decision to review came amid mounting pressure from the Black community to secure the successful prosecution of the three accused and at present that could not be guaranteed

She goes into a rage.

VALERIE	I don't believe this.
WILLARD	Do. I knew something was wrong. I did dream John last night.
VALERIE	You did?
WILLARD	Yes and it was as if he was crying and pointing to something on the floor. When I look I couldn't see nothing. I looked back to ask him what did he want me to see and he was gone. I'll see you later

He leaves the house. She goes to the phone and calls Naveen

VALERIE	Naveen? Hello, listen have you heard ... you have.. What is that about then, in our meeting with the C.P.S last week they assured us that with Peter now accepted as the main witness, the case was watertight.. What are they talking about serious doubts?........ Need more witnesses? For what?
NAVEEN	Valerie I'm here. Willard let me in

Naveen enters the house

VALERIE	Oh. This is outrageous. Peter has identified them several times...

NAVEEN   I know

VALERIE   I mean why do I have to read this in the paper, couldn't they have called or something. God what is wrong with these people.

NAVEEN   Valerie....

VALERIE   When will this thing come to an end Naveen?

NAVEEN   (*Trying to placate her*) When they stop protecting their own.

VALERIE   (*Bitter*) And who do we have to protect us eh? No one, that's why they treat us this way. Like nothings, nobodies. But I wont take this laying down, even if I have to die too, those boys are going to pay for killing my son

NAVEEN   Valerie if you are going to run this course and survive it you must expect these people to let you down at every juncture. The Police, the courts, the public.

VALERIE   And God?

NAVEEN   Valerie don't lose heart. I know right now it's hard to see but look at what you've achieved. Your lovely home, your successful business, things turn out right for you Valerie

VALERIE   What of my family Naveen? My daughters left home and we do not talk anymore, my youngest son, has run off to Grenada rather than live in the same house as me, I am married to a weak man who now practically lives around the house of the woman he has been seeing for the last twenty years. How right is that?

           At that point the fax machine starts to churn out a fax! Valerie goes to get it.

NAVEEN   All I know is that it's going to weigh in on our side

           At the same time there is a knock on the door and the sound of something being pushed through the letterbox.

NAVEEN   I'll get that for you shall I?

VALERIE   Yes thank you.

He goes to the front door. Valerie reads the fax

VALERIE God, these people have no concept of grammar.... *(She struggles to find the word)* 'Niggers you are worser than shit'

Naveen comes back into the front room. He is carrying a piece of turd on some paper. Valerie sees it.

VALERIE Well one can't say that they're not co-ordinated

NAVEEN I'll run out and see if any of the neighbours got the registration number

VALERIE I'll take that.

NAVEEN No. I'll deal with this.

He exits.

VALERIE John why is this happening? Is God laughing at me or what? It's as if he's making me into the parable of she who thought she had everything only to find out that she had nothing. Even you, John. You've come to every body else in dream but you don't come to me? Why? You don't think I need a encouragement too?

The lights come back up and Naveen comes back in on the phone

NAVEEN No good, no one saw anything except the couple next door and all they said was that the car was green. Hello, Inspector Graham Please. Yes.. Vandals just posted some excretion through the letterbox of the McKenna household. Along with a threatening fax ….Yes could you get some one over straight away. Thank you.

To Valerie

They'll be here in a wee while.

VALERIE Would you mind terribly if I was left alone.

NAVEEN Nonsense. This is no time for you to be on your own.

VALERIE *(Slightly strained)* I wouldn't make good company right now

He understands

NAVEEN Ok. I'll call by later. Tell the police they can call for my statement

He leaves. When it is clear that he has left the house Valerie sobs. After a few beats Jaime enters

Valerie instantly pulls herself together.

JAIME   I didn't know you'd be in

When she hears Jaime voice she spits out venomously

VALERIE   What do you want?

JAIME   (*Almost apologetically*) I came to leave this for dad

She places a wrapped birthday present on the table.

VALERIE   Well you've left it.

When Jaime can see that her mother is not going to communicate with her she places the house keys on the table

JAIME   And to return these.

Without looking Valerie clocks them. Pauses for a second and she leaves the room without even looking at Jaime or the keys

Jaime understands now that her mother has washed her hands of her. She turns and leaves the house

SCENE THREE

We are in the families front room. Willard is dancing to his favourite soca calypso cassette. He is singing and whooping, busting his favourite moves.

WILLARD   (*Singing*) If I only hold you tonight it's thunder, I giving whole night, caressing you whole night, I giving you... (*Speech*) BOYYYYYY you still have the moves, them young people can't touch this...

He pretends he's dancing with a woman. The doorbell rings. Willard jumps up and answers it. Enter Peter in his Caribbean shorts suit, suitcases etc etc. Near Peter burst into full Grenadian lingo

PETER   So wha appen, England cold hit all you so bad that you can't open you mouth?

WILLARD	Pardon. You're early boy!
PETER	Got a lift from Gatwick. So what, you can't say hello?
WILLARD	What happening bwoy?
PETER	Well I dere. Happy birthday old man (*Gives him a bottle of Rum*)
WILLARD	Thank you thank you. What, well you is real Grenadian now wee
PETER	Well what else I is? I could hear that you enjoying you self
WILLARD	Boy, all I need is me Soca tape and a little home rum on me birthday and I is happy. Well for a while at least
PETER	Till you realise that you to old do bust the moves that you use to
WILLARD	What!?! You could match me for moves?
	Smiles
PETER	Yes, any day of the week.
	Willard puts the cassette on again and bursts a move that he was doing earlier.
WILLARD	Boy you drunk? You young people don't know moves. Watch this
	Peter stands amused
PETER	Eh eh! But you to old to do this though
	He winds down to the floor and up again. Willard starts to laugh
WILLARD	Bwoy you bad!
PETER	I know!
	Acknowledging defeat he switches off the stereo
WILLARD	You know looking at you now reminds me of when you lot was little and we use to dance together.
	Laughing as he recalls

Remember how good Jaime use to move. The family use to look and say, but wait that chile is a West Indian.

Beat

PETER   Where's mum?

WILLARD   Out on some march or the other with Naveen. She is going to cuss you.

Peter doesn't answer

WILLARD   How was it? How was home sweet home?

PETER   Wicked Dad, just wicked

WILLARD   You like the young girls down there, more importantly did they like you?

PETER   Of course the girls in your village liked me. I was Mr. prim and proper young English as they called me

WILLARD   Boy I hope you did leave the people them girl children as you find them?

PETER   What! Like you use to?

WILLARD   That is a different subject

PETER   Yer yer, any way people were overjoyed at the mention of your name. They would cook for me, give me drinks, well the first one anyway, after that they expected English to pay for the rest of the night. I wonder where they got that idea from? No wonder you go home every decade. You'd be bankrupt the way you spend money.

WILLARD   Boy you have to spend money otherwise people think that you do all these years in the cold for nothing. Remember it was a simple trade off, sunshine for money, they provide the sunshine, you the…

PETER   Not me spending my money though, I didn't have it for that. Aunty Anniseata, sends all of her love, and a big frozen Lambi, I don't know what you guys see in that thing it's horrible.

WILLARD   You English people know anything about food, hush your mouth

PETER   I'm not English thank you.

WILLARD	So what you's West Indian?
PETER	I'm African dad, like we all are
WILLARD	I'm not no African, I'm a Grenadian
PETER	Well we'll see about that, anyway your old friend Time sent you a bottle of Rum, and Bam sent you some seamoss, I hope all this stuff hasn't stained my clothes you know.
WILLARD	Bam, boy that was a character. You know why he was called Bam?
PETER	No
WILLARD	Because he use't to knock man out with one punch. Man that boy did like to fight. If you were going to a dance in another village, every one would give him a dollar each just for him not to come. But if he did guarantee there'd be bacchanal.
PETER	That's why he said to me that if I got into any trouble I should call him and he'd sort it out.
WILLARD	At his old age, Bam should rest heself. Tell me about we family na

Peter stares into his eyes

PETER	Dad, I have said some harsh and horrible things to you over the last year and I'm sorry.
WILLARD	Never apologise for what you meant. But thank you. So, home?
PETER	Well I discovered the exact location of the plantation your great great great Grandfathers owned <u>and</u> slaved on. The funny thing is, I didn't feel the memory of that time in the land, in the island as a whole actually. It was as if the earth had forgotten. Anyway I found some distant family in that area. They told me some stories. Wow. Apparently the woman who married your great great grandfather, had put a curse on him. If he wouldn't be with her, he would never be able to live with another woman in peace, and what happened, you told me that your granddad never lived with his wife, he simply went there in the day and returned to his mothers at night
WILLARD	But I don't believe in that obea thing.

PETER   Believe in it or not this woman said that no McKenna has ever been able to live with his wife since. That shit frightened me.

WILLARD   Watch your mouth boy

PETER   Shit isn't a swear word!

WILLARD   All right. Carry on anyway.

PETER   I went back to the library and eventually was lead to Alexander McKenna plantation books. He had a whole page about the buying of his brother George. Now this is the exciting part. George McKenna our gtgtgtgrandfather, was a single man when he was bought, but married the daughter of a freshly imported African, named Coffee.

WILLARD   Who was named Coffee his wife or the African?

PETER   His wife was called Angnes; her father was called Coffee. Listen to this dad, Coffee was simply the Anglicisation of the Ghanaian name Kofi, spelt K.o.f.i. Meaning born on a Friday. Dad do you know what that means, your gtgtgrandmother was Ghanaian, her father came over on the slave ship 'Forever tomorrow' summer of 1799. Dad I have got us back to Africa.

WILLARD   My God, that's fantastic. How do you know all of this information is true?

PETER   Oh I've got the birth certificates and copies of the ledgers, everything. I've even done a chart so that we all can see. Dad this is a glorious day.

Willard looks at the chart

WILLARD   Wow. So what do you gonna do with this new-found information?

PETER   Dad I don't want you take this the wrong way but I've decided to change my name. I'm now on I'm going to be called Kwaku Kofi

WILLARD   Boy don't think that I am being negative but even if we did come from Africa once, we are not African now, and they'll tell you that themselves son. I don't want you to go down a road that may lead to disillusionment.

PETER   I understand that dad, but this is a new day, we don't have that African West Indian thing going any more.

WILLARD Really

PETER It's like for the first time since John died I'm beginning to find some peace. When I was in Grenada I felt part of something

WILLARD Ain't that the truth

PETER All that rage has gone Dad. I feel as if I was put on this path to find myself.

WILLARD Well then you do that son, but remember you have the benefit of being the first generation of West Indian children that can legitimately say "this country is mine. Don't waste that"

Peter looks at the state of the house.

PETER The place looks rough. What's been happening?

WILLARD It's been rough. The CPS has actually dropped the charges against the three boys due to lack of evidence they say. Further to that, the boys say the only reason that you have identified them as the killers, is because you'd had an argument with them the night before, got into a fight and lost. They have witnesses to prove this.

PETER Are you crazy, I'd never seen them in my life before that night

WILLARD Well that's not what they're saying.

PETER I attacked them, that's ridiculous

WILLARD I know

PETER They're just using me to get off the charges

WILLARD Uh ha.

PETER Nooo, Dad that can't be right

WILLARD Who said anything about right

Peter is fuming

PETER Na, these people are bloody taking the piss. I gonna have to do something about this. This has to stop. Those boys ain't getting away with this again

WILLARD   Something like what? You could take the law into your own hands?

PETER   That's exactly what I'm talking about doing!

WILLARD   Don't be stupid that's just what they want you to do?

PETER   Is it?

WILLARD   Yes it is. Haven't you just told me about this new peace you've found?

> *We hear the front door close. Enter Valerie. She walks in and ignores the men. She looks around the room. Peter cools somewhat*

PETER   Hello Mum, I've just heard about.....

> *She walks into the kitchen. Peter looks to his father. He looks to the floor as if to say that it's been that way of late. We hear Valerie slamming the pot covers.*

VALERIE   So if I don't cook you mean no one can find their way to the kitchen?

> *It sounds now as if the pots are being thrown onto the floor*

VALERIE   I have to be the man and the woman in this house, go to work, come home, go to the grave, go to the meetings, go to the police, go to the lawyers, me. I'm the only one inside here that can do anything? I mean what kind of men am I surrounded with?

> *We now hear plates being smashed up*

How can I come home after a long day's work and find dirty plates in the sink? This is outrageous. The people inside this house think that this must be a bloody hotel. Eat shit and do as you please, but me the arse will cook clean and serve for them? Well you lie, things around her are going to change, believe me.

> *She walks out of the kitchen and into the front room. Peter stands*

VALERIE   Do you live here?

PETER   Yes

VALERIE	Then how come the day before your leaving, you choose tell me that you're going home?
PETER	You were so busy and I...
VALERIE	You what? You have no blasted manners that's what

He starts to get a little annoyed

PETER	It was an impromptu thing
VALERIE	Did you not stop to think that as the trial was approaching we would need you here?

His tone increasingly irritated

PETER	Well it's not happening now is it? So what's the problem?

Valerie slaps him in his mouth

VALERIE	Don't use that tone with me young man, you understand.

Peter puts his hand to his mouth. It is bleeding. The blood rushes to his head but he calms himself

WILLARD	Valerie!

Slow with deep meaning

PETER	Don't, ever do that again mum.
WILLARD	The boy didn't deserve that
VALERIE	You shut your mouth, if you were any type of man you would have done it. But as usual you fulfil your brief, weakness
WILLARD	I wish you wouldn't take out your rage on us
VALERIE	What do you know of rage Willard? You think you see rage yet. Rage is what I feel when I look at you see my dead sons face in yours and realise that he was more man than you will ever be. When I see how incapable you are of doing anything about my sons death I am outraged

Willard turns to Peter

WILLARD   Boy go and clean your mouth

> *Peter slowly turns and leaves the room*

VALERIE   It has taken the death of my son for me to see you as you really are. Your weakness disgusts me. I am holding this thing up by my self, me Willard. I am the one at the meetings I am the one facing all of the pressure alone, alone Willard. Where are you? For Christ sake he was your child too, why are you not sharing this with me

> *Overlapping each other*

WILLARD   Because I'm tired god damn it, I am tired Valerie. All of us aren't made of the stuff that you are.

VALERIE   You think that I'm not tired too? That's a lame excuse

WILLARD   It's not an excuse. I don't want my photographs taken Valerie

VALERIE   You think that I do?

WILLARD   I don't want people whispering as I walk past them in the supermarket, that's the father of the boy that get murder you know... Don't him have a White child too!

VALERIE   What are you talking about, it happened!

WILLARD   (*Shouting*) I know it happened, but I don't want to live it every day of my life.

VALERIE   (*Shouting back*) That's because you're a coward

WILLARD   I don't care. I want my life back Valerie. John is dead and God knows I want those that did it to pay, but I can't take this. Now I admire your strength, but I don't have it, and I'm not going to live what I am not.

VALERIE   (*With meaning*) You coward. Every time I look at you, I feel sick.

WILLARD   I'm sorry to hear that.

VALERIE   You suit each other, you and that woman. Any person who can sit waiting for you for twenty years is a loser

WILLARD   Some might say it takes strength?

VALERIE	Yes fools. Why don't you just leave and go and live with her full time?
WILLARD	You'd like me to do that wouldn't you, take what ever blame there is for this sham we call a marriage, huh I'm not going to give you the pleasure. I don't hate you, and when I look at you I don't feel sick, I just feel sorrow for a woman who is so racked with pain that she can not longer see the wood for the trees
VALERIE	I don't want your sorrow. I don't want your sorrow. I'm going to sell the house
WILLARD	Isn't it our house?
VALERIE	No Willard it's my house and I'm going to sell it. Some of us are responsible for loans, campaigns, legal fees the lot
WILLARD	Isn't that why Elm house is for sale?
VALERIE	Yes, and now this one is too.
WILLARD	You know what Valerie, do what you want, I'm too tired to fight anymore. I'm going somewhere where I can find a little peace
	He picks up his jacket and leaves the room
VALERIE	Give her my love won't you.
WILLARD	I will
	Peter enters the room after Willard has left. He wants to talk to Valerie but is not sure how to approach her. He has a gift in his hand. He still is annoyed about the slap but is trying to fight that mood off
PETER	Mum
VALERIE	Yes
PETER	I bought this back for you. It's not much but well, it's the thought that counts isn't it
VALERIE	(*She takes it from him*) Thank you
	Silence. Peter heads for the kitchen

VALERIE   Where you going?

PETER   To clean the kitchen

VALERIE   When you've smashed something up, you want the time to savour the destruction. Leave it, when I'm ready I'll do it.

He turns around. Valerie very matter of factly

VALERIE   So did you have a good time?

PETER   It was excellent.

VALERIE   Good

PETER   I thought of you a lot when I was out there

VALERIE   Really? What about?

PETER   About some of the stories you use to tell us as children.

VALERIE   Oh not you as well

PETER   I kept thinking about the time when I asked you how we got to the West Indies, I must have been about six or seven, and you said that we were angels that flew all the way from Africa. However when we landed in Grenada for a rest, we saw the mortals eating salt and decided that we should too. But we ate too much, and it weighed us down so badly that we lost the ability to fly back. And that meant that we had to stay there forever.

VALERIE   Did I say that?

PETER   Yes, and I've never forgotten it.

VALERIE   Boy the rubbish you tell children just to shut them up

PETER   I don't think that was rubbish, I think you were right. Maybe that's why we are here now, paying the price.

VALERIE   What sin could we have committed so bad, that we have to face the crap we face now eh?

PETER   Maybe we gave up being angels by being too much like the mortals?

VALERIE   We were never angels child

The fax machine rings. Valerie collects the fax.

VALERIE   Oh my god. One of the old ladies at the home has had an accident.
           This what I mean about me having to do everything.
           She gets a sharp pain in her chest.

VALERIE   Ahhhhhhh

PETER   What mum?

Easing out of the pain

VALERIE   Nothing. It's just wind.

PETER   Are you sure?

VALERIE   Yes. Lets get one thing straight young man. I have not forgiven
           you for your behaviour. Don't get too pally pally with me you hear?
           If I tell you I'm all right, then I'm all right.

PETER   I see.

VALERIE   Pass me my jacket

PETER   A wise man once said to me 'What's the point in fighting for the
           dead and killing those who are living?

VALERIE   Sometimes those who are dead have more life in them.

She puts on her coat and exits the stage.

SCENE FOUR

*We are back at the McKenna household. It is ten p.m. We hear the
front door bell going ten to the dozen.*

*Valerie enters the space in her dressing gown.
The bell keeps on ringing. She gets a little worried. She decides to
call Naveen.*

VALERIE   Hello Naveen, I'm so sorry to call you at this hour but I'm on my
           own and someone's at the front door. I'm not expecting anyone. Ok
           see you soon.

Valerie approaches the door

VALERIE   Who is it? I won't answer unless I know who it is so you can ring all night.

JAIME   Valerie it's me, please open the door.

Valerie realises that it is Jaime but does not move.

JAIME   It's cold and wet out here. Please

Valerie slowly undoes the chain and bolt and opens the door. Valerie quickly walks back into the front room. Jaime enters a little after her. She is soaking wet and looks freezing. Valerie switches on the light. The place is a tip.

VALERIE   You look a mess.

JAIME   Do I?

VALERIE   Yes you do.

She looks at her then leaves the room for a moment and comes back in with a towel.

VALERIE   Here.

JAIME   Thank you

She takes it and starts to dry her hair. She attempts to explain her presence

JAIME   I was walking past the house and as it was a year since John.. I just didn't want to walk past and not say hello

Valerie doesn't say anything at first

VALERIE   Well you've said it now!

JAIME   Don't be cold with me Valerie, I really need you not to be cold

Silence

VALERIE   (*Still with out warmth*) You gonna just sit there in your wet clothes?

JAIME   I don't have anything else to put on

VALERIE	Use some of your fathers I'm sure he won't mind. I'm going back to bed. Let yourself out when you're ready.
JAIME	I'm thinking about trying to find my birth mother, what do you think?

Valerie looks at her sharply

VALERIE	The one that left you on the steps of the hospital?
JAIME	Yeah!
VALERIE	If you think you need to do that go ahead. I've no more pain to get from you Jaime.
JAIME	I don't want to give you pain. You're the only one that can answer…
VALERIE	Go to your birth mother na. You and her is same people right?
JAIME	Why did you adopt me Valerie?
VALERIE	Since when have you and I been companions child?
JAIME	Pardon?
VALERIE	Since when do you address me as Valerie?
JAIME	(*Jaime loses it*) Since you stopped being my mother

Unbeknown to Valerie and Jaime. Peter enters the house and stand watching the women argue

VALERIE	You walk out of this house, you walk on your family and then you have to nerve to tell me that I stopped being your mother? How dare you. You West Indian children are too damn fast with yourselves?
JAIME	Listen to you. West Indian! You know what I think. I think you adopted me because you wanted to fuck me up the way they've fucked up West Indians
VALERIE	Don't come in here and swear at me

JAIME — After what you have done to me you have a cheek. You have messed me up Valerie. That's the truth. I'd have been better off left on the steps

VALERIE — That's the thanks I'm gonna get? You ungrateful little…

JAIME — You see, you see. They shouldn't have allowed it Valerie. You purchased me. You only wanted me to show the world that you're as good as them. That's the truth isn't it?

VALERIE — How dare you accuse me of that?

JAIME — I'm not accusing you,

VALERIE — Jaime go, if you have come here to provoke my soul go. Come out.

JAIME — I came here for help because I need answers and all you tell give me is come out me house? Aren't you tired of that one yet?

Flashes of temper

VALERIE — No I'm not. This is what I have. I've paid for it with sweat and blood and Gods grace. Get out of my house. Go and find the bitch that gave birth to you na. See if because you and her share the same blood if you have anything else in common.

Peter enters the room. Calmly and coolly he say's

PETER — You heard my mother, Come on Jaime,

VALERIE — What are you doing sneaking up on people?

JAIME — (*To Peter*) I just came here to talk

VALERIE — To cause confusion you mean

PETER — My mums asking you to leave

JAIME — Peter.

PETER — That's not my name. Now Jaime before I have to physically remove you from this house, please leave.

JAIME — You wouldn't put your hands on me, not in the house I grew up in?

PETER — Yes I would

Valerie gets a sharp pain in her chest. She holds it. She suddenly loses all strength in her legs and falls to the floor.

JAIME   Are you all right?

PETER   Mum!

VALERIE   (*To Jaime*) As if you care. Stop you all stupidness. I'm all right

JAIME   You don't seem right to me Valerie.

VALERIE   Listen don't let me have to tell you people again that I'm….

She gets another seizure. She screams and falls back to the ground

JAIME   Oh my god.

Peter and Jaime stand paralysed for a moment

JAIME   Mum? Mum? Can you hear me?

Valerie doesn't respond. Jaime checks pulse and breath

PETER   Is she alright?

JAIME   I don't know, pass me the cushion. Quick

PETER   I'll call an ambulance. Hello could I have an ambulance please at 25 Grantham Rd.

At this point Naveen and Willard enter

NAVEEN   I think she was worried there might be an intruder

They see Valerie

WILLARD   What's happened?

JAIME   She just collapsed. Peters called an ambulance.

WILLARD   I'll get a duvet

JAIME   Ok mum, were gonna make you comfortable.

Naveen walks away and dials a number on his mobile.

NAVEEN   Hello, news desk... Yes hello, this is Naveen Patel, representative of the McKenna family. Yes well Mrs. McKenna

PETER   Ambulance is on it's way

NAVEEN   ...has just had a heart attack, an ambulance will be here soon, maybe you might want to get some photographers down here?

Jaime screams at Naveen

JAIME   Naveen you can't, that's disgusting, it's no time for the press

NAVEEN   I'm afraid it is Jaime. Why do you think she got this heart attack? The world needs to know. It'll help our cause

JAIME   Tell him he can't get the press over to see mum like this

NAVEEN   Hello Newsdesk, Yes hello, this is Naveen Patel, representative of the McKenna family...Yes well Mrs. McKenna has just had a heart attack, an ambulance will be here soon, maybe you might want to get some photographers down here?

Jaime leaves her mothers side and runs up to Naveen attempting to take the phone away from him.

JAIME   Give me that phone, I said give me that phone

As they struggle. Willard puts the warm towel on Valerie forehead.

JAIME   I'll not have you prostitute her like this

Naveen explodes

NAVEEN   Can you not see that what I am doing will help? This kind of media attention can only bring weight to bear on the authorities. They put her here! We need to show them that. If Valerie were conscious, she would want to me do this. Guys, I need you more than ever right now to see the big picture?

JAIME   Naveen there are lines of decency that should not be crossed. This is one of them.

NAVEEN   Justice is dirty work. We are taking here about the straw to break the juries back. We'd miss this opportunity why? Because we didn't have the courage to seize the day I couldn't live with myself if that were to happen?

Peter takes the phone from Jaime and hands it to Naveen. As he is exiting the house we here him back on the phone

NAVEEN   Hello, is this the newsdesk? Yer, If I were you I'd get your photographers here as soon poss. Valerie McKenna has just had a heart attack. Ambulance is on it's way.

He slams the door on his exit. We hear the sound of the ambulance approaching. Jaime goes back to her mothers side.

JAIME   They're coming mum, everything will be all right.

LIGHTS OUT.

SCENE FIVE
We are in the front room of the family home. Most of the furniture is packed away in boxes or covered over. The house has been sold and they are ready to move. Jaime wheels her mother on in a wheelchair. Valerie has a note pad and pen, and a handkerchief to wipe the side of her mouth with. Her voice sounds very weak and she paralysed on one side. She can hardly speak.

JAIME   Everything's packed up and the removal men will be here soon

Valerie looks at her child. She looks sad.

VALERIE   You're father

JAIME   He phoned from the court, he said everything was everything. They should be here now but then again you never know with those two

Beat. She doesn't answer

JAIME   Tomorrow all these years of memories will be gone. Our spirit won't own the new house. When I walk into the front room I wont see dad dancing to his Soca tapes, John cooking in the kitchen... Mummy I so want to wave a magic wand and have everything the way it was.

Enter Willard

JAIME   Hi dad. How did it finish in court today?

WILLARD   Ok I think. The prosecution will complete tomorrow, then we go see.

JAIME   Where's Peter?

WILLARD   Kwaku

JAIME   Sorry Kwaku

WILLARD   Parking the car. Everything ready to leave?

Jaime nods. He walks up to Valerie

WILLARD   How are you today Val?

She nods her head

VALERIE   Fine.

She attempts to continue but Willard stops her

WILLARD   Don't try to talk Val, write it down.

She starts to slowly write. Enter Peter. We can see he's a distraught young man. He sees Jaime, they greet each other cordially

JAIME   Hey Kwaku

PETER   Jaime

He bends over and kisses Valerie on the forehead. She feels his pain more than ever.

VALERIE   How's it looking?

PETER   Don't you worry mum I've got everything under control. I've set up an all night vigil at outside of the court tonight, they'll be demonstrations all day tomorrow from Peckham to Tottenham. The jury will have to find them guilty or else they'll be...

VALERIE   .....Sssssshhhhhh (*Valerie cuts him off and indicates to him to go and get*) Your fathers rum

WILLARD   How you know where I does hide me rum?

Valerie attempts to kiss her teeth.

VALERIE   I Dream John.

WILLARD   You did?

Valerie smiles from cheek to cheek.

WILLARD   That's great Val.

Peter returns with the rum. She beckons Willard over to her and gives him the rum and note pad

VALERIE   Bless the house

He reads Valerie's words at first while sprinkling some rum around the house. But after a sentence or two he stops and continues from his heart

WILLARD   Dear lord any wrongs that I may have done, remove them from the path of my family. Rebuke the hate, confusion, lies and denials that have beset us. Heal us. Be with us as we leave this place. And whatever family inherits this house, let them find the peace we once had.

He finishes the libation. They're ready to leave.

WILLARD   You ready?

Valerie nods her head. He fixes her coat and they turn and exit the house.

The End

Big Nose was co written By Christopher Monks

The first performance took place at the Belgrade Theatre Coventry 2nd September 1999
The cast were as follows:

Clovis Dibiset	Kwame Kwei-Armah/Derek Elroy
Rosemary	Julie Saunders
Hubert Lafayette	Louis Decosta Johnson
Du Bois/Chief/Vincent	Malcolm Fredrick
Miss Baptiste/Celia/Paula	Sharon D Clarke
Gladstone/Peter	Nicholas Beveney
Lord Sugarcoat	Joseph Jones
Governor/Philpot	Howard Gay
Panny/Pastor Macwilliams	
Tennant/Derek	Dale Superville
Actor/Musicians	Guy Holden, Ian Riley, Errol Kennedy and Joe Paterson

And a community cast of ten playing townspeople, carnival dancers, revellers, choristers and tenants

Directed By	Chris Monks
Designed by	Patrick Connellan/Cathy Ryan
Musical Direction	Akintayo Akinbodi
Lighting Designer	Dolly Henry
Fight Director	Renny Krupinski

PART ONE

ACT ONE

FEBRUARY 1958.

THE CONCERT HALL OF AN EASTERN CARIBBEAN ISLAND.

UPSTAGE IS A BAND STAND DECORATED WITH UNION JACKS AND PICTURES OF THE QUEEN. DOWNSTAGE ARE TWO AREAS FOR V.I.P. GUESTS. IN ONE SITS THE GOVERNOR IN THE OTHER, DU BOIS, A RESPECTABLE MIDDLE-AGED 'BUSINESSMAN' AND HIS HEAVY: GLADSTONE. OTHER SEATS ARE OCCUPIED BY PEOPLE OF THE ISLAND.

AS THE LIGHTS COME UP A CALYPSO IS IN PROGRESS PERFORMED BY LORD SUGARCOAT, THE M.C., AND MISS BAPTISTE BACKED BY A CALYPSO BAND COMPRISING BASIE, PANNY AND HUBERT.

SUGARCOAT WEARS HIS TRADEMARK PANAMA MADE OF SUGAR CANE.

BIG NOSE ! - ACT ONE

OH, CALYPSO

OH CALYPSO,
CALYPSO,
THE SONG IS FAST, IT MAY BE RUDE
ITS THE MOUTHPIECE OF THE MULTITUDE.
CALYPSO,
CALYPSO,
CAN HELP A POLITICIAN WIN
THEN SLAP HIM BACK TO EARTH AGAIN.

THE CALYPSONIAN BANISH YOUR BLUES
THEM BRING YOU THE GOSSIP, THEM SING YOU THE NEWS
FEEL THE BEAT INFECTING YOUR SHOES
ITS A WEST INDIAN RYTHM YOU CAN'T REFUSE

OH CALYPSO,
CALYPSO,
THAT CRAZY CELEBRATION
THE POETRY OF THE POPULATION
CALYPSO,
CALYPSO,
IT BUILD THE POLITICIAN UP
THEN MAKE HIM DRINK THE POISON CUP

THE CALYPSONIAN SATIRIZE
THE HYPOCRITES WHO WE ALL DESPISE,
OR SING THE PRAISES OF THE BRAVE AND WISE,
LISTEN WHILE THE MASTER EXTEMPORISE:

I SAID CALYPSO.
CALYPSO,
THE CHAMPION OF THE DESTITUTE
DRESSED UP IN THE SHARPEST SUIT
CALYPSO,
CALYPSO,
THE POLITICIAN GLORIFIED
THEN BOOTED UP HIS BIG BACKSIDE.

SONG ENDS

BIG NOSE ! - ACT ONE

SUGARCOAT   Thank you, thank you, thank you! Miss Baptiste of
            Baptiste's Dumplin' Shop. I don't really agree
            with woman Calypsonian on the stage, but she bribe
            me with her sweet Johnny Cakes. Now, get back to
            the kitchen.

MISS B   You're damn rude.

            SHE STORMS OFF

SUGARCOAT   Is joke I'm makin', joke I'm makin'
            My Lords, gentlemen and ladies, thankyou for
            patronizing our establishment this evening.
            On this the fifth celebration to the ascension of
            our beloved Queen Elizabeth the first,...er, the
            second to the trone. I am your M.C.for tonight Lord
            Sugarcoat 'The Original Calypsonian'.

            LOUD STRUPS. EVERYONE LOOKS ROUND SEES NOBODY.
            SUGARCOAT THINKS IT IS THE BAND.

            (TO BAND) Come off the stage now, big people
            tings.

            HUBERT AND BASIE LEAVE THE STAGE, PANNY SITS AT THE
            PIANO.

            (TO AUDIENCE) As you can see we've had a wealth of
            local talent.tonight, but now it is my esteemed
            pleasure to begin to introduce....

            A BEAUTIFUL YOUNG WOMAN IN HER LATE TEENS CROSSES
            TO TAKE HER SEAT WITH DUBOIS. HUBERT, THE DRUMMER
            FROM THE CALYPSO BAND, BUMPS INTO HER. THEIR EYES
            MEET.

            Oh what a pleasure it is to see the most beautiful
            Miss Rosemary in the prescence of our sponsor for
            tonight Mr.Du Bois, of Blue Stripe Breweries. So
            everybody stand up and give this wonderful
            benefactor a round of applause.

            HE LEADS A ROUND OF APPLAUSE. DUBOIS ACKNOWLEDGES
            THE CROWD. A JINGLE PLAYS AS A LARGE CUT OUT BOTTLE
            OF BEER CROSSES THE STAGE.

VOICES   *IF YOU WANT THE CATS TO MIAOW AND MOAN*
            MAKE SURE YOU PACK A STRONG BONE.
            WOOF! WOOF!

            As I was saying, before I was so wonderfully
            distracted, it is my pleasure to introduce to this
            esteemed audience the celebrated Trinidadian Tenor,
            Mr.Ronald Fernandez. The first song of his
            repertoire tonight is the song......

BIG NOSE ! - ACT ONE

        HE HAS TO REFER TO HIS PROGRAMME

        ...'Santa Saint Lucia'.(Loo-sha)

FERNADEZ   (OFFSTAGE) Lucia ! (Loo-chee-a)

SUGARCOAT   Santa Lucia!

        A LARGE TENOR IN EVENING DRESS ENTERS, FULL OF HIS
        OWN IMPORTANCE. POLITE APPLAUSE ESPECIALLY FROM DU
        BOIS. GLADSTONE WHOOPS IT UP, DU BOIS LOOKS
        ASKANCE. PANNY PLAYS THE INTRODUCTION.

FERNANDEZ   *SUL MARE LUCCICA*
            L'ASTRO D'ARGENTO.....

        A VOICE SHOUTS FROM THE AUDIENCE.

VOICE   Jack Ass. Didn't I tell you not to come back 'ere
           wid dat shit!

        FERNANDEZ COUGHS. PANNY PLAYS INTRO AGAIN AND
        FERNANDEZ CONTINUES.

FERNANDEZ   *SUL MARE LUCCICA*
            L'ASTRO D'ARGENTO.....

VOICE   Back side! You don't hear me, you deaf?
           Of course you are, tone deaf, because:
           No man with an ear for melody,
           Sensitivity or humanity,
           Could release such a cacophany
           Except Fat Boy Ronald Fernandez.

DU BOIS   Don't let him intimidate you, carry on !

VOICE   Anyone in here who is name man,
           Let them stand and contradict my plan   !

        GLADSTONE STANDS DUBOIS HOLDS HIM BACK. LORD
        SUGARCOAT TIMIDLY CREEPS ON.

SUGARCOAT   People have paid....

VOICE   Do you want a cut-arse ?

SUGARCOAT   (TO THE CROWD) We're givin' no refunds.

        IN FEAR OF HIS HEALTH, SUGARCOAT LEAVES THE STAGE.
        DU BOIS STANDS UP DEFIANTLY.

DU BOIS   Sing on !

BIG NOSE ! - ACT ONE

VOICE
: Sing on! If you wish each note to be
  Further provocation for me,
  To whip and beat you like a swine,
  And with each squeak and with each whine,
  Multiply the shame you feel
  With words and rythms that are real.

FERNANDEZ
: To insult me is to insult Orpheus !

GOVERNOR
: Hear! Hear!

GLADSTONE
: Who is dat?

ROSEMARY
: The Greek God of Music.

  CLOVIS SWINGS DOWN ONTO THE STAGE WITH A GUITAR STRAPPPED TO HIS BACK. PANNY LEAVES THE PIANO AND PICKS UP HIS GUITAR.

CLOVIS
: Gods! Whose are these gods you worship ?
  You talk to me of Greeks!
  You sing to me in Italian!
  You've bastardised, europeanised
  A thing that was once pure and true,
  And that is why, fat sir,
  I will always exorcise you !

  CLOVIS TRIES TO GRAB FERNANDEZ HE RUNS FOR HIS LIFE. THE AUDIENCE CHANTS:

AUDIENCE
: We want to hear the song!
  We want to hear the song!
  We want to......

CLOVIS
: ....I challenge any man in here to say I'm wrong !

  SILENCE

  Just as I thought.

  THE GOVERNOR HAS LEFT HIS SEAT AND IS ABOUT TO LEAVE.

GOVERNOR
: This is a disgrace! How dare you disrupt this occasion, it's an insult to Her Majesty's Government.

CLOVIS
: Before you go, sir:
  Here's a fact for contemplation:
  It's nineteen fifty-seven now
  We have our Federation,
  The West Indies comes of age !
  And takes its rightful place
  Upon the international stage......

GOVERNOR
: You may have your West Indian Federation, young man but its still part of the Empire, and your allegiance is to Queen Elizabeth and the Crown !

BIG NOSE ! - ACT ONE

CLOVIS
.....A close union of all the Isles
Where English bureaucrats have got piles...
...Of Money, at our expense,
But no more, we've now seen sense.
We can run our own affairs
Because for your government: no one cares!

THE GOVERNOR LEAVES DISGUSTED.

DU BOIS
Show dat boy who is man inside here.

GLADSTONE
It'll be my pleasure, Mr. Du Bois.

DU BOIS LEAVES TO CATCH UP WITH FERNANDEZ.

ROSEMARY
Gladstone, you've never beat him yet.

GLADSTONE
There's a first time for everything and I feel I've got the crowd behind me.

ROSEMARY COVERS HER EYES AS GLADSTONE CONFRONTS CLOVIS.

GLADSTONE
Personally, I thought your song was trash!
I'd rather listen to Fernadez than you.

CLOVIS
Bein' the damn fool dat your are, did you even understand a syllable of what that man was singin' about ?

GLADSTONE
Clovis, you tink you're bad, in'it ?

CLOVIS
Well that depends on your definition of bad, doesn't it fellow?

CLOVIS STARTS TO LEAVE.

GLADSTONE
Well, my definition of bad is your big nose!

CLOVIS STOPS IN HIS TRACKS

ROSEMARY
Eeh - eeh!

CLOVIS
Oh no. You know you shouldn't have said that !

BAND RUSH TO PROTECT THEIR INSTRUMENTS.

CLOVIS
When you could've said....

HE STARTS TO PLAY THE SONG. AS IT DEVELOPS EVERYONE JOINS IN THE CHORUS.

BIG NOSE ! - ACT ONE

BIG NOSE

CLOVIS
    WHAT YOU THINK YOU'RE DOIN', YOU GREAT BIG HUNK,
    WALKIN' ROUND WITH THAT ELEPHANT'S TRUNK ?
    BIG NOSE, YOU WID THE GREAT BIG NOSE!

    WHEN THE BRITS GOT BOMBED BY ADOLF HITLER,
    THEY USE YOUR NOSE FOR AIR RAID SHELTER.
    BIG NOSE, YOU WID THE GREAT BIG NOSE!

    HURRICANE SEASON, MIGHTY BREEZES,
    DATS WHAT HAPPEN WHEN CLOVIS SNEEZES.
    BIG NOSE, YOU WID THE GREAT BIG NOSE!

    GLADSTONE CHARGES CLOVIS WHO NEATLY CATAPULTS HIM
    INTO THE AUDIENCE.

    YOUR BOGIE SO BIG THAT ONE AND ALL
    USE THEM TINGS AS A CRICKET BALL.
    BIG NOSE, YOU WID THE GREAT BIG NOSE!

    EVERY NIGHT YOU GOTTA SEAL UP THE HOLES
    OR GET INFESTED WITH BATS AND MOLES.
    BIG NOSE, YOU WID THE GREAT BIG NOSE!

    GLADSTONE CHARGES AGAIN THIS TIME HE ENDS UP IN THE
    WINGS.

    YOUR MOTHER LAUGHING LIKE A HYENA,
    SHE USE YOUR NOSE AS A VACUUM CLEANER.
    BIG NOSE, YOU WITH THE GREAT BIG NOSE!

    SIGN UP FOR THE ARMY AS A SHOOTER:
    DON'T NEED A RIFLE, JUST USE YOUR HOOTER.
    BIG NOSE, YOU WITH THE GREAT BIG NOSE!

    CLOVIS USES HIS GUITAR AS A SHIELD TO PARRY A BLOW
    FROM GLADSTONE, A CHORD SOUNDS. GLADSTONE HOLDS
    HIS HAND IN PAIN. CLOVIS PUTS DOWN HIS GUITAR.

CLOVIS
    Mmm Eb! You know,
    To beat you, yet again,
    Would be an easy exercise,
    But here lies my challenge:
    While I extemporise
    Rhymes so subtle
    And verses so sweet,
    I'll knock you out boy
    When my song's complete,

    PAUSE

    On the final beat.

BIG NOSE ! - ACT ONE

AN EXPEDITION WENT IN TO SEE
JUST HOW DEEP WAS THE CAVITY.
IT WAS SO DARK THEY STARTED TO PANIC,
THEN THEY CAME UPON THE LOST TITANIC.
THE LEADER SAY: 'YOU MUST ACT LIKE MEN
OR YOU NEVER SEE YOUR WIFE AND CHILDREN AGAIN'.
THEY WENT IN SO DEEP, WENT IN SO FAR,
THEY CAME OUT ON THE COAST OF ZANZIBAR.

I SAY
BIG NOSE, YOU WID THE GREAT BIG NOSE!
BIG NOSE, YOU WID THE GREAT BIG NOSE!

CLOVIS KNOCKS GLADSTONE OUT ON THE LAST BEAT OF THE SONG.

SONG ENDS. MORE CONGRATULATIONS FOR CLOVIS.

BIG NOSE ! - ACT ONE

          THE CROWD GATHER ROUND THE UNCONSCIOUS BODY OF
          GLADSTONE. AS SHE LEAVES WITH MISS BAPTISTE,
          ROSEMARY PRESSES A NOTE INTO CLOVIS' HAND.

SUGARCOAT   Ladies and gentlemen, I'm sure you will agree you've had a knock-out evening! Dat punch remind me of when Joe Louis, 'The Brown Bomber', dropped one on Max Schmelling! Before we depart for our respected properties, can we stand, place our hands on our hearts and sing our national anthem.

          'GOD SAVE THE QUEEN' PLAYS AS THE LIGHTS FOCUS ON
          CLOVIS READING ROSEMARY'S NOTE.

ROSEMARY'S VOICE
          'Dear Clovis, meet me at your Auntie's dumpling shop, tomorrow at twelve noon. I have urgent matters of the heart I need to discuss with you. It cannot wait another day, your friend, Rosemary.

          THE ANTHEM ENDS. LIGHTS BACK TO NORMAL.
          A MEMBER OF THE BAND, BASIE, APPROACHES CLOVIS.

BASIE   Whoa boy! Eh man congratulations, Clovis.

CLOVIS   Basie, If you got a letter from a woman saying 'I have urgent matters of the heart to discuss with you and it cannot wait another day' what would you think?

BASIE   Simple, I would think she want me.

CLOVIS   But what if she could have any man that she wanted.

BASIE   Well, whoever she is, it look like she want you.

          BASIE SLAPS HIM ON THE BACK

          And Sugar Boy, don't stay out all night: we rehearsing at twelve tomorrow. By the way I've found us a new drummer, he's called Hubert. He from St.Croix, but he's not bad.

          ENTER A POLICEMAN AND THE CHIEF OF POLICE SEEING
          GLADSTONE STILL UNCONSCIOUS.

CHIEF   What the hell going on here !

CROWD   Bacchanal !

          GLADSTONE RECOVERS CONSCIOUSNESS

P.C.   (EXCITEDLY) Bacchanal where !?

SUGARCOAT   Felix boy, everyting done, don't worry yourself !

BIG NOSE ! - ACT ONE

CHIEF   I keep tellin' you Sugar, when we outside the family house don't call me by mi name. We've been given information from a very reliable source of a civil disturbance.

GLADSTONE   Dat's right. Arrest dat man !

CHIEF   On what charge ?

GLADSTONE   Murder! He tried to murder me !

CLOVIS   The only murder that was goin' on in here was the murder of Caribbean culture. Ronald Fernandez was the guilty party so I dismissed him from the stage.

CHIEF   On whose authority ?

CLOVIS   On the authority of good taste.

CHIEF   Clovis Dibiset, I dun warned you so many times about your stupidness, dis time you've gone too far. In my capacity as Chief of Police I'm goin' to have to arrest you for disturbing the peace.

THE CONSTABLE TAKES OUT SOME HANDCUFFS WITH GLEE. CLOVIS STARTS TO SNIFF THE AIR.

GLADSTONE   Lock 'im up and trow away di key ! The man is a menace !

CLOVIS   Wait, wait !

CHIEF   I'll have no back-chat!

CLOVIS   No seriously, I smell burnin' ! Somewhere on the island there's a big fire.

CHIEF   Well I can't smell anyting ! Anybody else smell anyting ?

NO ONE CAN

GLADSTONE   He tryin' to fool you.

CLOVIS   When it comes to sensitive nostrils I'd say I was uniquely qualified.

HE SMELLS THE AIR AS DOES EVERYONE ELSE. CLOVIS GETS A BEARING.

It's North of Freetown.

AT THIS MOMENT MISS BAPTISTE RUNS INTO THE HALL WITH THE CHIEF'S FIRE HAT.

BIG NOSE ! - ACT ONE

MISS B　　　　　Inspector, inspector we looking for you everywhere
　　　　　　　　The whole of North Freetown is on fire ! Clovis'
　　　　　　　　the fire headin' for the Orphanage !

　　　　　　　　CLOVIS LEGS IT. THE CHIEF CHANGES HATS.

CHIEF　　　　　In my capacity of Fire Chief...everybody grab a
　　　　　　　　bucket and run.

　　　　　　　　EVERYONE LEAVES THE STAGE SHOUTING 'FIRE'.

END OF ACT I

ACT TWO

THE NEXT DAY.
MISS BAPTISTE'S DUMPLING SHOP, JUST BEFORE NOON.

THE STAGE IS DIVIDED IN TWO. DOWNSTAGE A DOOR LEADS TO THE STREET, NEXT TO IT A COUNTER BEHIND WHICH ANOTHER DOOR LEADS TO THE KITCHEN. STAGE RIGHT THE BAND'S INSTRUMENTS ARE SET UP FOR THE REHEARSAL.

AS THE LIGHTS COME UP MISS BAPTISTE IS BRINGING FOOD INTO THE SHOP. SHE BEGINS TO SING.

DURING THE SONG THREE MUSICIANS ENTER:
BASIE, HUBERT, AND PANNY. THEY JOIN IN THE CHORUS.

BIG NOSE! - ACT TWO

IN PRAISE OF DUMPLING

MISS.B.
WHEN YOUR BELLY PLEADIN'
THERE'S SOMETHIN' THAT ITS NEEDIN'
YOU KNOW WHERE YOUR BELLY SHOULD LEAD YOU
DON'T NEED NO DIPLOMA,
JUST FOLLOW THE AROMA,
THIS IS WHERE YOUR AUNTIE GO FEED YOU.
DON'T LOOK FOR NO FROGLEGS OR PASTA
NO SPANISH OMELETTE OR FRANKFURTER

DUMPLING! BOY, THEY'RE REALLY SOMETHING
DUMPLING! LET ME TELL YOU ONE THING
YOU CAN FRY IT, YOU CAN BOIL IT,
YOU CAN BAKE IT, BUT YOU CAN'T FAKE IT.
YOU CAN FRY IT, YOU CAN BOIL IT,
YOU CAN BAKE IT, BUT YOU CAN'T FAKE IT.

BAND
DUMPLING! HOW WE LOVE WE DUMPLING,
DUMPLING! HOW WE LOVE WE DUMPLING,

MISS.B.
YOU CAN KEEP YOUR CAVIAR
YOUR CHAMPAGNE OR YOUR ADVOCAT
THERE IS NOTHING SWEETER THAN DUMPLIN'
IT FILLS ME WITH ELATION
TO FOLLOW MY VOCATION
AND SATISFY THE NATION WITH DUMPLIN'
HOW THAT THING TASTES NICE WHEN IT FRY
IT SWEET WITH PEAS GUNGO OR BLACK-EYE.

ALL
DUMPLING! BOY,THEY'RE REALLY SOMETHING
DUMPLING! LET ME TELL YOU ONE THING
YOU CAN FRY IT, YOU CAN BOIL IT,
YOU CAN BAKE IT, BUT YOU CAN'T FAKE IT.
YOU CAN FRY IT, YOU CAN BOIL IT,
YOU CAN BAKE IT, BUT YOU CAN'T FAKE IT.

BAND
DUMPLING! HOW WE LOVE WE DUMPLING,
DUMPLING! HOW WE LOVE WE DUMPLING,

SONG ENDS

BIG NOSE! - ACT TWO

PANNY Any chance of some food, Miss Baptiste ? My belly's rumblin' like a cement mixer.

MISS B. Just give me two minutes boys: you can't expect to sing sweetly on an empty stomach.

SHE ENTERS THE KITCHEN

BASIE Hubert, you better fix up your drums, he'll be here any minute, and we always start bang on time!

HUBERT I hear he have a foul temper.

BASIE What, he crazy, but he's the best. Don't let me down, right. Oh yes, most importantly, whatever you do don't mention his.....

HE TAPS HIS NOSE

CLOVIS ENTERS DISTRACTED PUTTING THE FINISHING TOUCHES TO A SONG LYRIC.

CLOVIS What time is it ?

BASIE Time to start, is only you we waitin' for.

MISS BAPTISTE RETURNS WITH FOOD FOR THE BAND. CLOVIS SITS AT A TABLE WRITING

CLOVIS Auntie, what is the time ?

MISS B. Five to twelve, boy.

PANNY We got five minutes. Tell us what happened last night, the whole island's talkin' about how you singlehandedly save Freetown from the fire.

BASIE And how you knock out Gladstone.

PANNY Magnificent!

CLOVIS (CURTLY) The rehearsal is postoned today come back in half an hour !

NO ONE MOVES.

PANNY But we want to hear about how you beat up the fire.

CLOVIS I said, vamoose, mash!

CLOVIS PUSHES THEM OUT OF THE SHOP.

MISS B. What's wrong with you!

CLOVIS Nothin'

BIG NOSE! - ACT TWO

MISS B. Clovis, you're actin' very strange. What's the matter? Let me see that burn on your arm.

CLOVIS No, no, no its fine.

HE PICKS UP THE LETTER AND MOVES AWAY FROM HER.

Auntie, I can stand and sing in front of a thousand people; a whole town burnin' down doesn't scare me, but I am more nervous now than I have ever been. The woman I have secretly loved all my life has asked to meet me here in...what is the time ?

MISS B. Almost twelve.

CLOVIS In less than one minute the most beautiful woman is going to walk through the door to meet me.

MISS B. And...?

CLOVIS Look at me.

MISS B. Yes, you have a big nose, but every other thing about you is worthy of praise. I know I curry favour but, before too long they'll be writing calypsos about you.

CLOVIS Dat may be so, but will it include the word love.

THE DOOR OPENS AND IN WALKS ROSEMARY.

ROSEMARY Good afternoon, Miss Baptiste.

MISS B. Hello, Rosemary, you're looking radiant.

CLOVIS CATCHES ROSEMARY'S EYE. THEY STARE AT EACH OTHER SPEECHLESS FOR A MOMENT, SHE WITH ADMIRATION, HE WITH LOVE.

CLOVIS Yes, you are.

ROSEMARY INDICATES TO CLOVIS TO GET RID OF HIS AUNT.

CLOVIS Auntie, didn't you say you had some shopping to do?

MISS B. No.

CLOVIS You know, the fresh fish you said that was comin' in today.

DAWNING REALISATION

MISS B. Oh de fresh fish, me did forget about today's catch You know what I like about those fisherman they're so **bold** ! (SHE WINKS)

MISS BAPTISTE LEAVES THEM ALONE IN THE SHOP.

BIG NOSE! - ACT TWO

ROSEMARY   You are a brilliant man !

CLOVIS   I am ?

ROSEMARY   Yes, you know you are. You struck a victory last night when you embarrassed Du Bois. How I hate that man.

CLOVIS   How could your father make such a wretch your guardian ?

ROSEMARY   Well, I'll be free of him soon.

PAUSE

CLOVIS   Don't you sometimes long for the time when things were simple.

ROSEMARY   Yes. When we were kids. You used to come and visit your cousins and when my father was out you'd sneak into our house with your guitar, I'd stop practising Mozart on the piano and we'd sing rude calypsos.

SHE SITS AT THE PIANO AND SINGS

COCK-A-ROACH IN MI PETTICOAT

CLOVIS   *CLIMBING HIGHER AND HIGHER*

THEY LAUGH

ROSEMARY   And then after...

CLOVIS   ...I'd climb the trees to get the coconuts....

ROSEMARY   ...and I'd search for fallen mangoes. We'd fill we

BOTH   .. belly til we were sick!

ROSEMARY   Do you remember the time that gang of roughnecks accused me of stealing their dog and were about to beat me, when you ran in and cut each and everyone's backside so bad, til all today every time they see me they tilt their hat and say m'am ?

CLOVIS   I remember.

ROSEMARY   You've always protected me, Clovis.

SHE SPOTS HIS BANDAGED ARM.

But, what's wrong with your arm?

BIG NOSE! - ACT TWO

CLOVIS   A small burn from the fire last night.

ROSEMARY   Oh my God, I heard how you rescued those hundred children from the orphanage. What happened ? Tell me all about it.

            CLOVIS GETS OUT HER LETTER.

CLOVIS   We can talk about dat later. You tell me about these 'urgent matters of the heart'.

BIG NOSE! - ACT TWO

NO OTHER MAN

ROSEMARY
*I'D PICTURED A STUDIOUS LIFE,
AWAY FROM THE TEDIOUS STRIFE
OF GIRL MEETING BOY
AND THE ULTIMATE JOY
OF SPENDING MY DAYS AS A WIFE.*

*I'D HID IN THE DUST OF MY BOOKS,
AVOIDING THE LUSTIER LOOKS
OF MALES WITH A DIFFERENT AGENDA,
BUT NOW HOW I YEARN TO SURRENDER:*

*SO GOODBYE MR.SHELLEY,
FAREWELL MR.KEATS!
I FEEL IT IN MY BELLY,
MY FOOLISH HEART KEEPS SKIPPING BEATS.
GOT NO NEED FOR SHAKESPEARE,
BYRON OR JOHN DONNE,
THE THEORY IS OVER
AND PRACTISE HAS BEGUN.*

*NO OTHER MAN, CAN FIRE IMAGINATION.
NO OTHER MAN, CAN TRIUMPH OVER ART.
MY LIBRARY IS NOW A CONFLAGRATION,
HE TURNS A PAGE AND TEARS MY WORLD APART.*

*SO GOODBYE TO SPINOZA
AU REVOIR ROUSSEAU
THE BOOKISH LIFE IS OVER,
MY LOVER CALLS, I'VE GOT TO GO.
PHILOSOPHY AND PHYSICS
DON'T MEAN A THING TO ME.
MY SOARING SOUL HAS CONTRADICTED
LAWS OF GRAVITY.*

*NO OTHER MAN, AND THIS IS MY CONVICTION
NO OTHER MAN, WRITES POEMS WITH HIS EYES,
OUR ROMANCE IS NOT A WORK OF FICTION,
HE MAKES THE TRUTH ILLUMINATE THE SKIES*

CLOVIS JOINS HER, CONVINCED HE IS THE OBJECT OF HER DESIRES.

BOTH
*NO OTHER MAN, CAN FIRE IMAGINATION.
NO OTHER MAN, CAN TRIUMPH OVER ART.
THE LIBRARY IS NOW A CONFLAGRATION,
HE TURNS A PAGE AND TEARS THE WORLD APART.*

*NO OTHER MAN, NO OTHER MAN,
NO OTHER MAN, NO OTHER MAN.*

SONG ENDS

BIG NOSE! - ACT TWO

CLOVIS So you love this man ?

CLOVIS TAKES OUT HIS SONG LYRIC.

ROSEMARY It was confirmed yesterday at the theatre. He was so rythmical, so manly, so beautiful....

CLOVIS Beautiful ?

ROSEMARY Yes, beautiful. The most beautiful man I've ever seen. And the good news is he is auditioning for your Carnival Band today! Isn't it brilliant, you've got to give him the job. He'd be close to you, you could protect him and teach him.

CLOVIS Auditioning for me ? What's his name ?

ROSEMARY Hubert Lafayette. The drummer from St.Croix.

CLOVIS A small island drummer ?

ROSEMARY My spies tell me if he doesn't get the gig he'll leave the Island. Clovis, I'll lose the one love of my life.

CLOVIS How do you know you love him ?

ROSEMARY What are you talkin' about ? He looks like a god !

CLOVIS Have the two of you spoken ?

ROSEMARY No, each time I've seen him, he's been too shy.

CLOVIS But you don't know him ! This isn't like you. You love eloquence, intelligence, the man could be an ass, more foolish than... Gladstone!

ROSEMARY No, a woman's instinct's are never wrong. If he is stupid then I'll simply have to die an old maid.

PAUSE

CLOVIS So, you want me to give him a job, protect and defend this small island boy because you.....

ROSEMARY ...you are my friend. There's nothing better than friendship. Is there ?

CLOVIS No, I don't suppose there is.

ROSEMARY Then you'll give him the job?

CLOVIS Yes.

ROSEMARY Teach and protect him ?

BIG NOSE! - ACT TWO

CLOVIS   I will.

ROSEMARY   Clovis, I love you, you sweet fudge, you.

LOOKS AT HER WATCH.

I've got to go. I know he's not stupid Clovis. Get him to write to me. Oh, you haven't told me about last night. Don't forget to get him to write to me.

CLOVIS   Yes.

ROSEMARY   You hero: a hundred children. I must go. You love me like I love you, don't you ?

CLOVIS   Yes. I....

ROSEMARY   You must tell me about it. A hundred!

SHE IS GONE. CLOVIS IS LEFT ALONE.

CLOVIS   ....do love you.

MISS B.   (OFFSTAGE) Bye Rosemary.

MISS BAPTISTE ENTERS WITH FISH. SHE SEES CLOVIS IS DOWN. SHE GIVES HIM A HUG.

Boy don't mind dat. Next week, when you're crowned Road March King, the whole world will be your oyster.

CLOVIS   Dat's not enough.

MISS B.   You'll find love. Dere must be a woman out dere who like a big nose man.

BASIE STICKS HIS HEAD ROUND THE DOOR.

BASIE   Clovis, what goin' on boy ? We rehearsing or what ?

CLOVIS   Yeah, come man, come.

ENTER BASIE, PANNY, AND HUBERT

BASIE   Clovis, dis is Hubert Lafayette the drummer I was telling you about.

CLOVIS   (TO HIMSELF) It's him.

HUBERT   It's a pleasure for me to meet you, Mr. Executioner

CLOVIS   Where you from, boy ?

HUBERT   Saint Croix.

BIG NOSE! - ACT TWO

PANNY   Oh a small island. Calypso arrive dere yet ?.

                   PANNY GIGGLES

BASIE   Shut your mouth ! We want to hear about the fire, man.

PANNY   Yeah, before we rehearse we want to know how you rescued all those people.

BASIE   The whole town lookin' for you, you know boy.

                   PANNY JUMPS ON A TABLE WITH A GUITAR.

PANNY   I would just like to give a tribute to the hero of Freetown.

                   C IS THE CHAMPION OF FREETOWN,
                   L IS FOR HE WHO IS LOVE.
                   O HOW OUR HERO IS WEIGHED DOWN,
                   WITH BLESSINGS FROM ABOVE.
                   V STANDS FOR VICTORY IN EVERYTING HE DO.
                   I AM SURE THAT YOU WILL SEE
                   S STANDS FOR SUPER C.

BASIE   Super C ? What the arse is dat ?

PANNY   Super Clovis, you stupid or what !

BASIE   (TO CLOVIS)Tell us the story na, man !

CLOVIS   Awright, awright.

BIG NOSE! - ACT TWO

FIRE CALYPSO

CLOVIS
POLICE WAS GOIN' TO TAKE ME DOWN
WHEN I SMELL FIRE, NORTH OF FREETOWN
AT FIRST THEY DIDN'T WANT TO HEAR
BUT MY INTELLIGENCE IT TAKE THEM THERE
THE PLACE WAS PURE CHAOS
REAL HIGH FLAMES AND LOTS OF FUSS
I SHOUTED 'GET THE FIREMAN HOSE!'
PEOPLE SAID:....

HUBERT
USE YOUR BIG NOSE !

PAUSE. CLOVIS LOOKS AT HUBERT

CLOVIS
WHAT THEY SAID I WILL NOW DISCLOSE

THEY SCREAMED:
FIRE BURNIN' FIRE BLAZIN'
KICK DOWN THE DOOR, KICK DOWN THE DOOR
FIRE BURNIN' FIRE BLAZIN
KICK DOWN THE DOOR, KICK DOWN THE DOOR

A WOMAN JUMP FROM SHE WINDOW LEDGE
SHOUTIN': 'CHILDREN BURNIN' IN THE ORPHANAGE!'
LORD, TO HEAR A HUNDRED BABIES SCREAM
WAS WORSE THAN YOUR MOST HORRID DREAM.
ME THINK HARD AND EXECUTE MI PLAN
ME TAKE ME AXE IN ME HAND
I WET DOWN ALL MI CLOTHES
TAKE A DEEP BREATH........

HUBERT
THROUGH YOUR BIG NOSE !

CLOVIS
AND IN I GOES.

COS THE
FIRE BURNIN' (FIRE!) FIRE BLAZIN' (FIRE!)
KICK DOWN THE DOOR, KICK DOWN THE DOOR
FIRE BURNIN' (FIRE!) FIRE BLAZIN' (FIRE!)
KICK DOWN THE DOOR, KICK DOWN THE DOOR

MOST HUMANS COULDN'T TAKE THE HEAT
BUT THOSE CRUEL FLAMES I JUST HAD TO BEAT.
BY THE TIME I'D GOT TO THE SECOND FLOOR
I HAD SAVED MORE THAN NINETY-FOUR.
MAN, TO RESCUE THE OTHER SIX
THAT FIRE WOULD GIVE ME SOME TERRIBLE LICKS
BUT IN ME THE STRENGTH AROSE

HUBERT
AND YOU BLOW OUT THE FIRE WITH YOUR BIG NOSE !

CLOVIS
IT WAS LIFE AND DEATH, WHAT DO YOU THINK I CHOSE ?

HUBERT
TO PULL THE HAIR OUT OF YOUR NOSE !

THE SONG ENDS ABRUPTLY. CLOVIS IS IN A RAGE

BIG NOSE! - ACT TWO

CLOVIS   Out, out, out!

PANNY   Oh-ho, Cut backside!Somebody call de funeral parlour !

BASIE   (TO HUBERT) What the hell you playin' at!

          THEY RUSH OUT PUTTING A CLOSED SIGN ON THE DOOR. HUBERT STANDS READY TO PROTECT HIMSELF.

CLOVIS   You.... Come mek my hug you.

          CLOVIS HUGS HIM.

HUBERT   Huh!!!!!!!!!???????

CLOVIS   Boy you brave, I like a man who's brave. A man suppose to be brave.

HUBERT   I..I don't understand.

CLOVIS   I'm her brother.

HUBERT   Whose brother ?

CLOVIS   Hers !

HUBERT   Who are you talkin' about ?

CLOVIS   Her. Rosemary.

HUBERT   Oh, my God you're her brother ?

CLOVIS   Well, sort of. We been best friends all our lives.

HUBERT   And she's, and she's...

CLOVIS   Told me everything, yes ! She loves you.

HUBERT   She love me ! I can't believe it ! Oh, Lord, I'm so happy.

CLOVIS   Yes, I imagine you would be.

HUBERT   I'm so sorry about all that nose business, Mr. Executioner. You know you are my favorite calypsonian in the whole world.

CLOVIS   Call me, Clovis. She don't lie, you're a good lookin' man.

HUBERT   She love me! So, what I go do now ?

BIG NOSE! - ACT TWO

CLOVIS   Rosemary want you to write to her.

HUBERT   What??!!

CLOVIS   She told me to tell you, you must write her a letter tonight.

HUBERT   No, no, I can't.

CLOVIS   Why not ?

HUBERT   I'll mash up everyting.

CLOVIS   Why ?

HUBERT   I left school in 4th standard. I don't know nuttin' about letter writin'. I don't even know how to talk to a woman like her. I'm no good wid words.

CLOVIS   Rubbish. What about all that 'nose' business ?

HUBERT   That's just a man thing. A woman like her must likes poetry and ting and ting so. She's class. Men like you have words, but not me.

CLOVIS   I have the words but not the looks.

HUBERT   I have the looks but....

CLOVIS   Hubert, just tell me what you want to say and I'll write it down.

HUBERT   Awright! That's good, that's good.

                   PAUSE. HE GATHERS HIMSELF.

                   Rosemary you are the most beautifullist tings....

CLOVIS   No, no, you have to tell her what's in your heart. You have to....(AN IDEA DAWNS)...(TO HIMSELF)tell her what's in your heart.(TO HUBERT) Why not let me be your words? I'll write and you sign it.

HUBERT   Why would you do that ?

CLOVIS   Let's just say I'd rather see her with you, than that bloodsucker Du Bois.

                   TAKES THE LYRIC FROM HIS POCKET.

                   Here's a love song I wrote this morning. All you need to do is address it to her and you're on your way.

BIG NOSE! - ACT TWO

>   HUBERT TAKES THE LETTER AND WITH AN UNCONTROLABLE
>   JOY LEAPS ONTO THE DRUMS AND STARTS TO LAY DOWN
>   A WICKED BEAT.

CLOVIS   Dat's the rythm. Dat's the rythm. Boy where'd you
                get that beat ?

HUBERT   We small island boy have a little something, you
                know.

CLOVIS   Boys, come, come, come. This is the rythm for
                'Federation'.

>   THE BAND AND MISS BAPTISTE ENTER AND START PLAYING
>   ALONG.

THE WEST INDIAN FEDERATION

CLOVIS
INDIA AND PAKISTAN
WON INDEPENDENCE FROM THE ENGLISHMAN,
PEOPLE YOU'VE GOTTA UNDERSTAND
WE'RE GONNA DO THE SAME THROUGH THE CARIBBEAN!

TRINIDAD AND JAMAICA,(ST. KITTS)
BARBADOS AND GUYANA, (NEVIS)

THE WEST INDIAN FEDERATION !
(END THE TRIBULATION)
THE WEST INDIAN FEDERATION !
(OF COLONIAL SUBJAGATION.)
THE WEST INDIAN FEDERATION !
TALKIN' 'BOUT THE BIRTH OF A NEW NATION,

TOWARDS THE END OF THE SONG DU BOIS ENTERS WITH GLADSTONE.

SONG ENDS.

BIG NOSE! - ACT TWO

THE BAND CONGRATULATE HUBERT.

PANNY   Boy, dat tune bad.

MISS B.   That go cause Baccanhal in the Carnival!

            DU BOIS APPLAUDS POLITELY.

DU BOIS   Interestin', interestin' very interestin'. It look
            like Lord Executioner do it again. Where you get
            that rythm from, boy ?

CLOVIS   (CURTLY) How can I help you ?

GLADSTONE   ...Mr. Du Bois to you.

CLOVIS   Would you like me to manners your poodle ?

DU BOIS   It's not how you can help me, it's how I can help
            you.

CLOVIS   Is dat so.

DU BOIS   Yes, this is all fine. But how do you fancy leading
            a real band ?

PANNY   Damn cheek !

MISS B.   Shhh!

DU BOIS   In next weeks Carnival I want you to lead the Du
            Bois Blue Stripe Strong Bone Band.

GLADSTONE   (SINGS THE JINGLE HOLDING UP A BEAR BOTTLE)
            IF YOU WANT THE CATS TO MIAOW AND MOAN
            MAKE SURE YOU PACK A STRONG BONE. WOOF! WOOF!

DU BOIS   With my band and your lyrics we'll win the 'Road
            March', 'Carnival King', 'Calypso Monarch': people
            will be namin' their babies after you, just think
            a million little Executioners ! What do you say ?

CLOVIS   I'd rather be bottom of the Carnival list
            Than lead the band of an ars...onist !

GLADSTONE   Don't talk to Mr. Du Bois like dat !

CLOVIS   Boy don't let me have to whup you again !

DU BOIS   Those are serious allegations young man, perhaps
            the heroics of last night have made your head a
            little giddy.

CLOVIS   I would not have to have been a hero, if
            someone hadn't skimped money on installing the
            orphanage electricity in the first place, making it
            a disaster waiting to happen !

BIG NOSE! - ACT TWO

DU BOIS   Really.

CLOVIS   My surroundings may be humble,
My band may be minimal,
But I'd rather die a pauper
Than represent a criminal.

DU BOIS   That can be arranged.

GLADSTONE   You a fool to yourself, don't forget Blue Stripe is sponsoring the Carnival.

CLOVIS   You're a fool if you think you can ride
Roughshod over a man with pride.
You're a man who has cheated and lied.
Would you really have been satisfied
If last night all of Freetown had cried
That a hundred young children had died ?

DU BOIS   Obviously I've come to the wrong man, but I'd be careful about casting aspersions, Gladstone let's go.

     THEY LEAVE. THE BAND CHEER CLOVIS.

MISS B.   Did you need to be so rude, Clovis? Remember he's one of the Road March judges.

CLOVIS   So what, we got the rythm, we got the tune.

MISS B.   He's a very powerful man.

CLOVIS   What can he do to me ? You don't see boat lining up everyday to take people to England ?

BASIE   Who wants to go to England ?

HUBERT   It's always been my dream to go to England. Go there, make some money, come back a rich man.

     CLOVIS HUGS HUBERT.

CLOVIS   Ah, I love dis fella. A man with vision.

BASIE   Eh - eh! What is this? He huggin' the boy. I thought you were gonna kill him.

PANNY   Me too. So, we can all call you Big Nose now !

     CLOVIS SMASHES HIM TO THE GROUND.
     BLACKOUT.

END OF ACT II

ACT THREE SCENE ONE

              THE MAIN STREET OF THE TOWN.
              THE CARNIVAL ROAD MARCH IS IN PROGRESS.

              DU BOIS AND HIS FELLOW JUDGES SIT WATCHING
              AS WE HEAR THE LAST FEW BARS OF 'THE BLUE STRIPE
              STRONG BONE BAND'

BLUE STRIPES   *IF YOU WANT THE CATS TO MIAOW AND MOAN*
              MAKE SURE YOU PACK A GOOD STRONG BONE
              WOOF! WOOF!

              DANCERS IN SPLENDID REGALIA MARCH DOWN THE STREET
              TO THE MUSIC OF THE LORD HIGH EXECUTIONER AND HIS
              BAND. THEIR COSTUMES REFLECT THE RESOURCES AND THE
              FLORA AND FAUNA OF THE CARIBBEAN.

BIG NOSE! - ACT TWO

THE WEST INDIAN FEDERATION (Reprise)

CLOVIS
GHANA HAS ITS FREEDOM NOW:
KWAME NKRUMAH HIM SHOWED US HOW.
LET US ALL TAKE A SOLEMN VOW,
AS THE EMPIRE TAKES ITS FINAL BOW.

MARTINIQUE BETTER KEEP IN TOUCH,
KICK OUT THE FRENCH! KICK OUT THE DUTCH!

THE WEST INDIAN FEDERATION !
(END THE TRIBULATION)
THE WEST INDIAN FEDERATION !
(OF COLONIAL SUBJAGATION.)
THE WEST INDIAN FEDERATION !
TALKIN' 'BOUT THE BIRTH OF A NEW NATION,

A LARGE EFFIGY OF UNCLE SAM WITH A VAMPIRE CAPE AND MANY ARMS ENTERS AND CREATES HAVOC AMONGST THE DANCERS.

SOME LEECHES IN OUR LAND,
BLEEDIN' DRY THE COMMON MAN,
BUT VAMPIRE GOT NOWHERE TO HIDE
WHEN THE CARIBBEAN UNIFIED!

DIRECTED AT DU BOIS

SUNRISE AND IT AIN'T NO JOKE,
HE'LL GO UP IN A PUFF OF SMOKE.

THE UNCLE SAM EFFIGY IS SWEPT FROM THE STAGE BY THE DANCERS

THE WEST INDIAN FEDERATION !
(END THE TRIBULATION)
THE WEST INDIAN FEDERATION !
(OF COLONIAL SUBJAGATION.)
THE WEST INDIAN FEDERATION !
TALKIN' 'BOUT THE BIRTH OF A NEW NATION,
THE WEST INDIAN FEDERATION !
(BUILT ON FIRM FOUNDATION)
THE WEST INDIAN FEDERATION !
(A CARIBBEAN CONGREGATION)
THE WEST INDIAN FEDERATION !
TALKIN' 'BOUT THE BIRTH OF A NEW NATION.

BY THE END OF THE SONG THE JUDGES ARE UP AND DANCING WITH THE CROWD, ALL EXCEPT DUBOIS, WHO OBVIOUSLY HAS OTHER IDEAS ABOUT THE OUTCOME OF THE CONTEST.

SONG ENDS

BIG NOSE! - ACT TWO

ACT THREE SCENE TWO

UNIT NINE

    LATER THAT EVENING IN A SQUARE BY THE HARBOUR, STAGE RIGHT IS ROSEMARY'S HOUSE: PROMINANT ABOVE IS HER BALCONY. UPSTAGE IS THE LOW WALL OF THE HARBOUR. CENTRE IS A CIRCULAR STONE SEAT SURROUNDING A SMALL MANGO TREE.

    ENTER CLOVIS WITH SUGARCOAT, BASIE AND PANNY SINGING AN ACOUSTIC REPRISE OF CLOVIS' CARNIVAL CALYPSO. THE MOOD IS CELEBERATORY.

SUGARCOAT   Clovis, though it burn me to say dis: you are the man. I take off my hat to you.

PANNY   Woahee, Sugarcoat takin' off he hat!

SUGARCOAT   No, no, never let it be said, I'm not a man who stands up to his responsibility. Clovis, I have long considered myself the originator, the most accomplished of Calypsonians, but that song you did at the Road March today has guaranteed your admission to the Pantheon of the Great Caribbean Poetic Geniuses.

PANNY   Yeah!

SUGARCOAT   Shut up, I don't finish yet. So, in short, boy you bad.

CLOVIS   (SLIGHTLY EMBARRASSED) Thank you. That means a lot to me, Sugar.

    HE SHAKES HIS HAND. CLOVIS REMEMBERS HIS ERRAND

    Any way, enough of this stupidness. Mash, move, I got things to do. I'll see you later back at the stand in time for The Executioner to collect his carnival crown.

    LAUGHTER AND CELEBRATION

BASIE   Yeah. So you not comin' to the War, Clovis ?

SUGARCOAT   You know Jungle Lion leaving on the boat for England tonight. If you don't come he's gonna think you're scared and take your title as Calypso Monarch with him.

BIG NOSE! - ACT TWO

CLOVIS   Listen, Jungle Lion's got his hands full with you and Genghis Khan. I go meet all you there. I have some business I have to do first.

THE BOYS LEAVE NOISILY.

<u>UNIT TEN</u>

CLOVIS TAKES OUT AN ENVELOPE APPROACHES ROSEMARY'S FRONT DOOR AND POSTS IT THROUGH THE LETTER BOX.

AS HE WALKS AWAY ROSEMARY APPEARS ON THE BALCONY.

ROSEMARY   Is that you Clovis ? Wait there, I'm comin' down.

ROSEMARY OPENS THE DOOR THEN NOTICES THE LETTER SHE PICKS IT UP SMILING. SHE DOES NOT REALISE HE HAS POSTED THE LETTER.

ROSEMARY   Clovis you were fantastic at the Road March today. You is The Executioner for true. Did you see Du Bois' face when you sang that line about 'Some Leeches in our land'.

CLOVIS   (HAPPY) I know, I know, I know. Not even he can deny me my crown. Did you see the way the other judges were dancing ?

ROSEMARY   As great as you are, you cannot touch the brilliance of my beautiful Hubert.

CLOVIS   Brilliance ?!

ROSEMARY   (WAVING THE LETTER IN FRONT OF HIS FACE)
Not a day goes by without him sending me another love song.

CLOVIS   Really ?

ROSEMARY   You have a way with words that makes wrong-doers tremble with fear. But Hubert talks of love and his lyrics provoke a different sort of trembling altogether! You should sit down with him and let him show you his style.

CLOVIS   Love, men don't talk about love.

ROSEMARY   Rubbish! A real man can be both tender and strong.

CLOVIS   How does he do that?

ROSEMARY INDICATES THE LETTER

ROSEMARY   Like this:

BIG NOSE! - ACT TWO

ISLAND QUEEN

ROSEMARY (SPOKEN) Love, how is it measured?
The quick beating of the heart
When he is about to depart?
The departure of bodily strength,
When they are at arm's length?
The longing when she's out of view,
Will he remain ever true?

ROSEMARY *MY HOME IS ADRIFT IN THE SEA*
AND BRIGHTER LIGHTS ALWAYS CALLING ME.
THE GODDESS OF FORTUNE AND FAME,
STOPS ME SLEEPING SOUND COS SHE CALLS MY NAME.
A SHIP IN THE HARBOUR LIES WAITING,
BOUND FOR A FAR DISTANT SHORE,
BUT I FIND MYSELF HESITATING:
COULD I LEAVE THE ONE I ADORE ?

I HAVE SEARCHED THE LAND
BUT I'VE NEVER SEEN
GIRL WHO CAN COMPARE
WITH MY ISLAND QUEEN
SKY ABOVE IS BLUE
SEA IS DEEP AND GREEN
NOT LOVELIER
THAN MY ISLAND QUEEN

BUT ONE DAY I HAVE TO DEPART
LEAVE MY ISLAND AND BREAK MY HEART
BE GONE FOR A YEAR AND A DAY
THOUGH FRIENDS AND FAMILY MAY BEG ME STAY
SO WHEN I HAVE MADE MY DECISION
I PROMISE I'LL ALWAYS BE TRUE
I'LL HOLD ON SO TIGHT TO MY VISION
YOUR MAJESTY WILL SEE ME THROUGH

I HAVE SEARCHED THE LAND
BUT I'VE NEVER SEEN
GIRL WHO CAN COMPARE
WITH MY ISLAND QUEEN
SKY ABOVE IS BLUE
SEA IS DEEP AND GREEN
NOT LOVELIER
THAN MY ISLAND QUEEN

BIG NOSE! - ACT TWO

CLOVIS (SCORNFULLY) Not bad.

ROSEMARY Not bad ! This is poetry. This is Art.

CLOVIS A little simple, methinks, but the structure's there.

ROSEMARY You jealous. Red eye you red eye !

CLOVIS Me! Jealous!

ROSEMARY Yes, listen to this:
'You move with grace, your voice has charms
Like symphonies by Bach or Brahms......'

CLOVIS Bach didn't write any symphonies..

ROSEMARY You know what he means !

CLOVIS You know all his lyrics by heart ?

ROSEMARY Every last syllable.

CLOVIS It look like Hubert sweet you for true.

ROSEMARY For true and for real. (NEW IDEA) Clovis get my love to visit me tonight.

CLOVIS Are you both ready ?

ROSEMARY I'll meet him by the harbour wall.

CLOVIS What time ?

ROSEMARY After the War of the Calypsonians. Ten o'clock Which reminds me, I'm late. Anyway, shouldn't you be there ?

CLOVIS No man. Them ting is beneath me. I have to prepare for my coronation.

ROSEMARY Remember you said that last year. Musn't count your chickens.

CLOVIS What! Believe me, if I don't win this year I'll fold the band and be out of here.

ROSEMARY But you can't do that, Hubert would leave the the Island.

CLOVIS It's not going to happen cos I'm going to win, And the reign of The Executioner will begin.

ROSEMARY Clovis, what's the time now ?

CLOVIS Eight-thirty.

ROSEMARY Hurry up and give my message to Hubert.

BIG NOSE! - ACT TWO

> SOUNDS OFFSTAGE OF THE CALYPSO WAR.
>
> CLOVIS EXITS. ROSEMARY RUNS TO THE HOUSE TO GET HER SCARF AS SHE SHUTS THE DOOR DU BOIS APPEARS FROM THE OPPOSITE SIDE OF THE STAGE.

DU BOIS: Rosemary, Rosemary, beautiful Rosemary.

> HE KISSES HER HAND

ROSEMARY: Good evening Mr.Du Bois.

DU BOIS: I've told you before, you're a big girl now, call me Ignatius.

ROSEMARY: I couldn't possibly, sir.

DU BOIS: And where are you off to in such a hurry ?

ROSEMARY: The Calypso War between Lord Sugarcoat and Jungle Lion.

DU BOIS: It's hardly fitting for the ward of a prominent citizen to attend such entertainments unaccompanied.

ROSEMARY: I'm meeting Winnie and Joan there.

DU BOIS: O.K. Well as a connoisseur of Calypso tell me, what did you think of the Blue Stripe Band ?

ROSEMARY: They were really good, but not as good as The Executioner.

DU BOIS: What?! That braggart Clovis Dibiset ! Anyway, it doesn't matter, he's not gonna win.

ROSEMARY: Why ? The crowd were going wild for him.

DU BOIS: It was the considered opinion of my associates, the Road March judges, that he was a little too vulgar.

ROSEMARY: But the Blue Stripe Band were singin 'Oh Doggy Hold Your Bone'!

DU BOIS: It's not what you say, it's the way you say it. Anyway, he's not going to win. At midnight we'll find out who has. Woof Woof ! (LAUGHS)

> ROSEMARY REALISES THE CONSEQUENCES OF CLOVIS' DEFEAT.

ROSEMARY: (ASIDE)Oh my god.(TO DU BOIS) Er...Ignatius have I ever thanked you for....looking after me since my father died.

BIG NOSE! - ACT TWO

DUBOIS — No, no no, you don't need to..,...

ROSEMARY — I didn't realise it til now, how fortunate I was to be raised by someone like you. The whole island loves you.

DU BOIS — And do you share that love ?

ROSEMARY — Because of my inheritance, when I marry I won't need a wealthy man. But I do find myself attracted to men who use power wisely.

DU BOIS — And I find myself attracted to intelligent young women who recognise the potency of the mature man.

ROSEMARY — What I like about you is, you look out for the people. You look after the people. You give them what they desire.

DU BOIS — Desire ? What do they desire ?

ROSEMARY — I just saw the way the people were jumping for High Executioner. Braggart he may be, but a man like you knows how to put the will of the people before petty pride. Tell me who wouldn't want to be with a man like that for the rest of their lives ?

DU BOIS — The rest of our lives is a long, long time.

ROSEMARY — I simply know the kind of man I could adore.

DU BOIS — Right, I see. I've just remembered I've got a very important meeting in the judges tent. I shall see you later, my dear.

ROSEMARY — Ignatius. Woof, Woof !

DU BOIS LEAVES ON A CLOUD OF ECSTACY. ROSEMARY RUSHES OFF THE OTHER WAY FOLLOWING SOUNDS OF THE CALYPSO WAR.

<u>UNIT TWELVE</u>

ENTER CLOVIS FOLLOWED BY HUBERT.

HUBERT — You're not listening to me Clovis.

CLOVIS — Listen man, shut your mouth, this is the theme: 'The Newness of Love'. No, no, no it should be about,'A man being tender and strong'. Ights ! Clovis you bad boy!

HUBERT — Clovis you don't hear me ! Am not doin it anymore !

CLOVIS NOTICES HUBERT IS HOLDING A GUITAR

CLOVIS — What's that ?

BIG NOSE! - ACT TWO

HUBERT   It's my guitar.

CLOVIS   But you're a drummer.

HUBERT   I know. But I've been practising. I think I can do it, by myself.

CLOVIS   Do what.

HUBERT   I can woo Rosemary by myself.

CLOVIS   Woo Rosemary by yourself ? Are you stupid! Course you stupid: you're from Saint Croix !

HUBERT   I'm just tired of using your words, your ideas, your, your,.....YOUR! I feel inspired tonight. She loves me Clovis, I know this now. Now she just has to love me for me. And tonight she will. I've written her a song.

CLOVIS   Don't do it, I beg you.

HUBERT   I'm doin it. I don't care what you say.

CLOVIS   She's used to a certain standard of lyric, a level of penmanship, there's no way she'll accept some piece of....

HUBERT   Stop ! (CONSCIOUS OF HIS RHYME)
You can't squash my confidence tonight.
I've written this song and I've written it right.

CLOVIS   I'm telling you this is madness. Don't come running to me when it backfires in your arse.

                EXIT CLOVIS IN A HUFF

                HUBERT LEFT ALONE PAINFULLY PRACTISES THE GUITAR SOUNDS OF THE WAR SUBSIDE FOLLOWED BY APPLAUSE.

                ENTER ROSEMARY SHE SPOTS HUBERT. HE SEES HER AND BECOMES EXTREMELY NERVOUS.

ROSEMARY   Hubert, you're here. Clovis found you.

HUBERT   Yes, he did.

ROSEMARY   I got your latest lyric today.

HUBERT   You did ?

ROSEMARY   It touched my heart.

HUBERT   It did ?

BIG NOSE! - ACT TWO

ROSEMARY   Yes, it did.

HUBERT   Did it ?

ROSEMARY   Yes!

            PAUSE

HUBERT   Er...well..I've another for you.

ROSEMARY   Sing it to me here and now. Let me hear for myself
            the passion, dare I say love, that it contains.

            ACCOMPANYING HIMSELF HUBERT SINGS HIS LOVE SONG.
            IT IS SO BAD THAT ROSEMARY HAS DIFFICULTY
            CONTAINING HER MIRTH.

BIG NOSE! - ACT TWO

I LOVE YOU

HUBERT
*I'VE MET A GIRL
MY HEADS IN A WHIRL
SHE'S LIKE A PEARL
GONNA BE MY GIRL*

*ROSEMARY I LOVE YOU
ROSEMARY I LOVE YOU
I'LL BE THINKIN' OF YOU
ROSEMARY
ROSEMARY I LOVE YOU
ROSEMARY I LOVE YOU
THERE'S NO ONE ABOVE YOU
ROSEMARY*

SONG ENDS

BIG NOSE! - ACT THREE

ROSEMARY (LAUGHING) You are so bright! That's the worst country and western song I ever heard. Stop teasing me. Sing me the real song.

HUBERT That was the song. That was it.

ROSEMARY Be serious now, come on.

HUBERT Maybe the first part, could be a little bit...you know....

ROSEMARY You're serious ! That's the tune?!
But where are the words that quicken my heart,
And make my head swoon ?

HUBERT Rosemary, I love you.

HE KISSES HER. ROSEMARY DOESN'T RETURN THE KISS. SHE MOVES OFF.

ROSEMARY What you doin' !

HUBERT Rosemary...I love you.

ROSEMARY So you've said, but where are the words...where's the eloquence, the poetry ?

HUBERT My love is making me stupid.

ROSEMARY Damn right ! Every young buck in town rushes me with that line: 'Rosemary, I love you'!

HUBERT Rosemary, listen....

ROSEMARY No, you listen ! I wanted to hear from your lips the sentiments I have read in your letters. When you've removed the knot from your tongue, come and find me. Goodnight.

SHE STORMS OFF INTO HER HOUSE SLAMMING THE DOOR HUBERT IS DISTRAUGHT.

HUBERT Arse, arse, arse !

ENTER CLOVIS APPLAUDING

CLOVIS Very well done. 'I Love You'. Work of genius some might say.

HUBERT Oh my god Clovis, help me.

CLOVIS Who me ? You have the wrong man.

BIG NOSE! - ACT THREE

HUBERT   Clovis I beg you. If you don't help me I go dead. You have to help me find a way to make her love me again.

CLOVIS   After you done mash up the ting. How'm I gonna do that ?

A LIGHT GOES ON IN ROSEMARY'S BEDROOM.

HUBERT   Look !

CLOVIS   Her window.

HUBERT   You have to teach me something now, on the spot.

CLOVIS   On the spot ? What can I do on the spot with a numbskull like you ?

HUBERT   You can do anyting, you're the greatest calysonian in the world !

CLOVIS   You takin' this thing for joke.

PAUSE.

But, you know I think we can do a little something. Stand infront the balcony and repeat every line I sing.

HUBERT   How do we start ?

CLOVIS   Call her stupidee ! Look throw the pebble up at she window.

HUBERT   Oo oo (Owl like) Rosemary Oo oo.

ROSEMARY ENTERS ABOVE.

ROSEMARY   Who's calling my name ?

HUBERT   Me.

ROSEMARY   Who's me ?

HUBERT   Me. Hubert. I must speak to you.

ROSEMARY KISSES HER TEETH.

ROSEMARY   I don't have anything to say to you. Come off mi land ! It's evident that you're a fraud.

HUBERT   What !

BIG NOSE! - ACT THREE

HOPELESSLY IN LOVE

        CLOVIS PLAYS THE GUITAR AND QUIETLY SINGS EACH LINE THEN HUBERT REPEATS IT.

CLOVIS	*FRAUD MADAM, I MAY JUST BE*
HUBERT	*FRAUD MADAM, I MAY JUST BE*
CLOVIS	*BUT ISN'T EVERYTHING COMPARED TO THEE*
HUBERT	*BUT ISN'T EVERYTHING COMPARED TO THEE*
CLOVIS	*YOU TO ALL - A DIVINITY*
HUBERT	*YOU TO ALL - A DIVINITY*
CLOVIS	*MADAM PLEASE ACCEPT MY APOLOGY*

HUBERT   What was dat ! Sing up man, I can't hear you.

ROSEMARY   Sing more.

             CLOVIS TAKES OVER

CLOVIS

I STAND BELOW, HEART OPEN WIDE
TO DISPLAY EMOTIONS THAT I CANNOT HIDE
JUST AS EACH WORD YIELDS TO GRAVITY
RAIN DOWN YOUR PITY ON ME.

I AM HOPELESSLY IN LOVE,
WITH THE ESSENCE OF LIGHT.
FOR I AM HOPELESSLY IN LOVE
FOR THE REST OF MY LIFE.
I AM HOPELESSLY IN LOVE,
CALL ME EXTRAVAGANT,
BUT YOU ARE TO ME
LOVE'S EMBODIMENT.

I AM SEIZED AND RACKED WITH FURY.
THIS LOVE KNOWS, NEITHER JUDGE NOR JURY,
SENDING EACH BODILY PART INTO A SPIN
NOT KNOWING HOW TO START OR WHERE TO BEGIN
EACH GLANCE STARTS SOMETHING NEW
A SONG, A POEM: WORDS THAT ARE TRUE
I TREMBLE AT THE THOUGHT OF YOUR TOUCH
TO THINK OF YOUR LOVE, IS TOO MUCH

ROSEMARY JOINS IN THE CHORUS

I AM HOPELESSLY IN LOVE
WITH THE ESSENCE OF LIGHT
FOR I AM HOPELESSLY IN LOVE
FOR THE REST OF MY LIFE
FOR I AM HOPELESSLY IN LOVE
CALL ME EXTRAVAGANT
BUT YOU ARE TO ME
LOVE'S EMBODIMENT

SONG ENDS

BIG NOSE! - ACT THREE

CLOVIS	(WHISPERING) Do you still think I'm a fraud ?
ROSEMARY	No, you've moved me. But why does your voice sound so horse ?
CLOVIS	Nothing that a touch of lemon grass won't cure.
ROSEMARY	I could brew some for you.
HUBERT	(COUGHS) Why thankyou, that would be very nice. I'll climb up.

HE TRIES TO TAKE THE GUITAR FROM CLOVIS.

CLOVIS	Too much too soon.
HUBERT	Clovis, you sweet her to the point where she is begging for it. Now gimme dat !

HE YANKS THE GUITAR OUT OF CLOVIS' HANDS

ROSEMARY	What was that ?
HUBERT	I just said 'Mash damn cat !' Miaou !
CLOVIS	No !
HUBERT	Yes !
ROSEMARY	What's going on down there ?
CLOVIS	I'm just grappling with myself.
HUBERT	Am I being too forward ?
ROSEMARY	No, I invited you.

HUBERT LOOKS TO CLOVIS. SLINGS THE GUITAR ON HIS BACK AND CLIMBS UP TO THE BALCONY.

HUBERT ATTEMPTS TO SPEAK. ROSEMARY PUTS A FINGER TO HIS LIPS.

ROSEMARY	No words.

THEY KISS AND SHE LEADS HIM INTO HER ROOM.

CLOVIS WANDERS DOWN TO THE HARBOUR WALL AND SITS LOOKING OUT TO SEA. ENTER MISS BAPTISTE.

MISS.B.	Clovis, where was you man, we miss you at the Calypso War. What's wrong ?
CLOVIS	Auntie, what is there on this island for me ?
MISS.B.	What're you talkin' about ?

BIG NOSE! - ACT THREE

CLOVIS   I wonder if I have any future here.

MISS.B.   What do you mean, you're just about to be crowned Carnival King.

CLOVIS   Yeah, yeah, yeah. But what does it mean. Big fish in a small pond. Auntie, how much money you got ?

MISS.B.   What on me ?

CLOVIS   No I'm talkin' serious money. I'm toying with the idea of England.

MISS.B.   Stop that foolishness.

CLOVIS   No, Auntie, but if I wanted to go would you lend me the money ?

MISS.B.   Of course I would. But as you're not goin' to do that stupidness, mi savings stayin' in mi pillow.

                  ENTER PASTOR MCWILLIAMS AND THREE CHORISTERS
                  SINGING A WEDDING SONG UNDER ROSEMARY'S BALCONY

CHOISTERS   *WHEN I COME BACK DARLIN' SAY YOU'LL MARRY ME*
                  I WANT TO SPEND MY LIFE WITH YOU
                  I'LL WEAR A BAND OF GOLD
                  FOR EVERYONE TO SEE
                  I'LL TELL THE WORLD IF YOU MARRY ME.

                  ROSEMARY COMES TO THE BALCONY IN HER DRESSING GOWN.

PASTOR   Miss Rosemary!

ROSEMARY   That was lovely, but who sent you ?

PASTOR   Are you Miss Rosemary ?

ROSEMARY   Yes.

PASTOR   Praise the Lord. I have in my hand a communication for you. Come down, in the name of Jesus, and receive it. Let me hear an Amen.

CHORISTERS   Amen.

                  ROSEMARY GOES IN.

PASTOR   Sister Baptiste, may the blessings of the Lord be upon you.

MISS B.   Pastor McWilliams.

BIG NOSE! - ACT THREE

PASTOR (SNOOTILY) Young Clovis. Are you still allowing the Devil to use and abuse the talents the Lord has given you ?

CLOVIS Pardon ?

PASTOR Sister Baptiste, I want you to beg the lord to forgive this relative of yours for participating in that extravaganza of lewdness, that jamboree of sin. In that celebration of .....

CLOVIS ....emancipation ?

PASTOR Carn...evil!

ROSEMARY AND HUBERT ENTER.

PASTOR Sister Rosemary, I've been charged with the responsibility of delivering this to you in the flesh.

HE GIVES HER A LETTER.

ROSEMARY Who's it from ?

PASTOR A very prominant person. The Lord's business no doubt.

HUBERT AND ROSEMARY TAKE THE LETTER TO ONE SIDE. CLOVIS CAN OVERHEAR.

ROSEMARY (READING)'My dear child,today when you mentioned the kind of man you would spend the rest of your life with, I hope you don't find me audacious but My trusted Pastor McWilliams is ready to perform the ceremony that will unite two great families forever. The man you have chosen to marry will dedicate the rest of his days to your happiness. Forever yours, Ignatius St.John Dubois'.(TO HUBERT) My god, he's coming to marry me.

HUBERT What! What are we going to do ?

ROSEMARY I don't know. Wait, why don't you marry me ?

HUBERT Me! er..er..No!

ROSEMARY Don't you love me ?

HUBERT Of course I do, but I have nothing, I am nobody. What could I give you ?

ROSEMARY You don't need to give me anything, I have everything we need.

BIG NOSE! - ACT THREE

HUBERT That's exactly it. How could I, a man, live off a woman ?

ROSEMARY Stop it ! If you love me, marry me. If you don't, Dubois will.

PAUSE

HUBERT Alright.

ROSEMARY Pastor we are ready for the ceremony. Mr.Hubert Lafayette of St. Croix has proposed marriage and I have excepted.

PASTOR But I thought Mr. Du Bois.... ?

SHOWING THE LETTER.

ROSEMARY Yes, you're right Mr. Du Bois has given his blessing to our holy union.

PASTOR Are you sure, I was under the impression...

THINKING QUICKLY AND READING FROM THE LETTER

ROSEMARY 'P.S. Please imform the good Pastor that for his willing co-operation in this matter a contribution of $500 will be donated to the Church of...

MISS B ...All Saints and Holy Trinity.

ROSEMARY All Saints and Holy Trinity.

PASTOR All Saints and Holy Trinity! Praise the Lord, what a great man. So few of the landed gentry have a heart the size of Mr. Du Bois. Give me an Amen.

CHORISTERS Amen

CLOVIS AND MISS BAPTISTE EXCHANGE LOOKS.

MISS.B. Could I have a word with you, Pastor.

ROSEMARY CROSSES TO CLOVIS

ROSEMARY Clovis, Du Bois will be here any minute.

CLOVIS Don't worry I'll head him off at the pass. Get me your father's old gardening hat and a table cloth.

ROSEMARY ENTERS THE HOUSE.

Pastor how long will ceremony be ?

PASTOR About fifteen minutes.

BIG NOSE! - ACT THREE

CLOVIS   Take out the sermon and a couple of Amen's that'll
                  make it five.

                  ROSEMARY RETURNS WITH THE THINGS

ROSEMARY   Thankyou Clovis.

                  SHE KISSES HIM ON THE CHEEK AND RUNS BACK INTO THE
                  HOUSE.

CLOVIS   He now consumes the feast that I have prepared.
                  Still I have one consolation: his lips will be
                  touching her lips, but my words have touched her
                  heart.

GLADSTONE   (OFFSTAGE) You're looking twenty years younger
                  Mr. Du Bois.

DU BOIS   I feel it, Gladstone, I feel it.

CLOVIS   I have work to do.

                  HE THROWS THE CLOTH OVER HIS HEAD AND PUTS THE HAT
                  ON HIS HEAD TO STOP IT FALLING OFF AND JUMPS DOWN
                  BELOW THE HARBOUR WALL PICKING UP BASIE'S DRUM AS
                  HE GOES.

                  ENTER DU BOIS AND GLADSTONE

DU BOIS   Gladstone, mi tie straight ?

GLADSTONE   It's not your tie you want to be worrying about.

                  THEY BOTH CHUCKLE. CLOVIS SLOWLY RISES ABOVE THE
                  WALL MAKING GHOSTLY NOISES AS HE APPEARS.

CLOVIS   Oooooo !

GLADSTONE   What the arse is that ?

DU BOIS   This is no time for carnival foolery, we're busy.

CLOVIS   (ADOPTING A STRANGE VOICE)
                  Busy ! Fool ! the operative words

OBEA SPIRIT SONG

CLOVIS
TELL ME WHAT IS THE YEAR, THE DAY, THE HOUR ?
OLD MAN WHERE DO I BE ?
YOUR FACE SEEMS FAMILIAR, TAKE ONE MINUTE WILL YER,
SIR, YOU RECOGNISE ME ?

DUBOIS
No, I do not.

CLOVIS
YES, THERE'S SOMETHING 'BOUT YOUR ENERGY
I HAVE TO TELL YOU, APPEALS TO THE EVIL IN ME
MY MEMORY STARTIN' TO CLEAR
OLD BOY, IT WAS FOR YOU THAT I WAS SENT HERE.

DUBOIS
What are you talkin' about. Go about your business.

CLOVIS
MR.DUBOIS IT'S BUSINESS I'M ON
AND FROM ME YOU MUST NOT RUN
YOU CANNOT MALINGER,
THAT RING ON YOUR FINGER
IS NO PROTECTION.

OH TO YOU I'M NOT NO MYSTERY
YOU'VE OFTEN CALLED ON MANY OTHERS LIKE ME
YOU'RE MORE THAN WELL AWARE OF THE PLAN
I WAS SENT TO YOU BY AN OBEA MAN

WHAT HAVE YOU DONE
TO WAKE UP THE SPIRIT OF A DEAD MAN
I HOPE YOU HAPPY AROUND DEMONS
COS TONIGHT WE A GO PARTY

GLADSTONE
Let's get out of here, Obea Spirit!

DUBOIS
Gladstone, don't leave me !

GLADSTONE LEGS IT. DUBOIS CROSSES HIMSELF

Don't leave me !

CLOVIS
CHECK OUT THE MOON HOW IT BRIGHT
ON THIS YOUR LAST CARN-EVIL NIGHT
HELL'S FURY IS IN FLIGHT
YOU GO SEE HELL BEFORE DAYLIGHT
IN YOUR DAY YOU DO MUCH BAD
MAKE MANY PEOPLE BROKE AND SAD
NEVER HAPPY WITH WHAT YOU HAD
WELL, TONIGHT I A GO SEND YOU MAD

BIG NOSE! - ACT THREE

CLOVIS *I AM THE SPIRIT OF YOUR EVILNESS*
YOUR LEWD WAYS AND YOUR GREEDINESS
BEFORE YOU DEAD YOU GO CONFESS
THAT TONIGHT YOU GET POSSESSED

WHAT HAVE YOU DONE
TO WAKE UP THE SPIRIT OF A DEAD MAN
I HOPE YOU ARE HAPPY AROUND DEMON
COS TONIGHT WE A GO PARTY

SONG ENDS ABRUPTLY

GLADSTONE RETURNS

BIG NOSE! - ACT THREE

CLOVIS | I think I've covered enough time. Shall we celebrate ?

DU BOIS | Celebrate what ?

CLOVIS | A marriage.

DU BOIS | I know that voice.

REMOVES HIS DISGUISE

GLADSTONE | I know that ......

CLOVIS | That's right Clovis from the noble house of Dibiset.

THE DOOR OF ROSEMARY'S HOUSE OPENS AND HUBERT AND ROSEMARY ENTER AND EMBRACE. MRS. BAPTISTE THROWS RICE OVER THE HAPPY COUPLE. PASTOR McWILLIAMS SMILES AS THE CHORISTERS SING A REPRISE OF THE WEDDING SONG.

CHOISTERS | *WHEN I COME BACK DARLIN' SAY YOU'LL MARRY ME*
I WANT TO SPEND MY LIFE WITH YOU
I'LL WEAR A BAND OF GOLD
FOR EVERYONE TO SEE
I'LL TELL THE WORLD IF YOU ......

DU BOIS | You....she....you!

HOLDS HIS HEART NEEDING THE SUPPORT OF GLADSTONE

Miss Rosemary.....

ROSEMARY | (SHOWING RING) Mrs. Lafayette.

SHE KISSES HUBERT AGAIN

DU BOIS | You think you're smart, huh. You played that song good, boy . Well you gonna remember it that is the song that lost you the Carnival Crown.

PASTOR | Mr. Du Bois I performed the ceremony as you requested sir, all praises to you, and thankyou for your generous donation.

DU BOIS | Shut your damn mouth, you stupid fool !

THE PASTOR AND CHORISTERS EXIT

HUBERT | What do you mean, 'lost the Carnival Crown' ?.

DU BOIS | Well, Lord High Executioner had won but after this escapade I'm guillotining that. Gladstone go and tell the judges.

GLADSTONE LEAVES

BIG NOSE! - ACT THREE

HUBERT   But, you can't do that.

DU BOIS   Oh yes, I can young man. And after I've finished you'll be lucky if you can get a job feeding fowls. Neither of you will ever play or lead another band on this island.

CLOVIS   Is that a threat ?

DU BOIS   No young man that is a promise. (TO HUBERT)I hope you enjoy living off your wife !

         HE EXITS.

HUBERT   (TO CLOVIS) What're we goin' to do ?

MRS.B.   Clovis, you can always work in the dumpling shop.

CLOVIS   And die ! No, you know what I'm gonna do.....I'm goin' to England. That's right, there's a boat tonight.

ROSEMARY   Tonight ?!

CLOVIS   In fact Du Bois has done me a favour, I know I can do something there. This place is too small for me. I have to get the boat tonight. Auntie,can I borrow that money ?

MISS.B.   Well, I don't have it on me.

CLOVIS   Run home and get it !

MISS.B.   Now Clovis, are you sure you're thinkin' straight about this ?

CLOVIS   I know what I'm doin'.Before you know it, I'm gonna come back with enough money to build you a palace.

MISS.B.   O.K. boy, wait for me here.

         MISS BAPTISTE LEAVES.

HUBERT   I'm comin' with you.

ROSEMARY   What !

HUBERT   I goin' with him.

ROSEMARY   You can't.

HUBERT   I have to. What am I goin' to do here ? How am I goin' to live ?

ROSEMARY   I told you, I have enough...

BIG NOSE! - ACT THREE

HUBERT   No, I can't live like that. Let me go to England, make something of myself and I can come back someone you can be proud of. Someone I can be proud of.

ROSEMARY   But the boat leaves tonight!

THEY LOOK TO CLOVIS WHO SHRUGS HIS SHOULDERS AND MOVES AWAY.

HUBERT   I have to go.

PAUSE. HUBERT MOVES AWAY. ROSEMARY CROSSES TO CLOVIS.

ROSEMARY   Make sure you look after him.

CLOVIS   I will.

ROSEMARY   Keep him away from other women.

CLOVIS   I won't need to do that.

ROSEMARY   Make sure he writes to me.

SHE RETURNS TO HUBERT

CLOVIS   That you can be sure of.

CLOVIS REMAINS APART FROM ROSEMARY AND HUBERT

BIG NOSE! - ACT THREE

ISLAND FAREWELL

ROSEMARY
*PARTING IS ONLY A SWEET, SWEET SORROW
IF THERE'S THE CERTAINTY, TOMORROW,
I'LL SEE YOUR SMILING FACE AGAIN*

HUBERT
*THOUGH I MUST LEAVE YOU HERE ALONE
I SWEAR THAT I'LL COME SWIFTLY HOME
BUT, SWEETNESS, I CAN'T SAY WHEN.*

ROSEMARY
*HOW CAN I BARE TO LET YOU GO?
DON'T FORGET I LOVE YOU SO.*

CLOVIS/HUBERT
*FAREWELL MY ISLAND,
FAREWELL MY SOUL*

CLOVIS
*THOUGH RICHES MAY AWAIT ME
YOUR BEAUTY I'LL EXTOL*

HUBERT/ROSEMARY
*THOUGH OCEANS SEPARATE US
WE WILL NEVER TRULY BE APART*

CLOVIS/HUBERT
*FAREWELL MY ISLAND
FAREWELL MY HEART.*

CLOVIS SAYS GOODBYE TO ROSEMARY

CLOVIS
*NEVER FEAR HE'LL WRITE TO YOU
I'LL KEEP HIM SAFE, I'LL KEEP HIM TRUE
TRUST ME, BELIEVE, I'M YOUR FREIND.*

ROSEMARY RETURNS TO HUBERT

CLOVIS
*I NEVER SHALL RETURN AGAIN,
SIX THOUSAND MILES WILL EASE THE PAIN
IN TIME I WON'T HAVE TO PRETEND.*

ROSEMARY
*RETURN TO ME, PLEASE PROMISE THIS
SEAL IT WITH A LOVER'S KISS*

ROSEMARY AND HUBERT KISS.

CLOVIS/ROSEMARY
*FAREWELL MY ISLAND,
FAREWELL MY SOUL*

HUBERT
*THOUGH TROUBLES MAY AWAIT ME
SUCCESS WILL BE MY GOAL*

CLOVIS/ROSEMARY
*THOUGH OCEANS SEPARATE US
WE WILL NEVER TRULY BE APART*

CLOVIS/HUBERT
ALL
*FAREWELL MY ISLAND
FAREWELL MY HEART.*

SONG ENDS

END OF PART ONE

PART TWO

ACT FOUR - SCENE ONE

THE RAIL OF A SHIP LINED WITH YOUNG WEST INDIAN MEN
DRESSED IN THEIR BEST. AMONGST THE CROWD ARE
CLOVIS, HUBERT AND PETER. THE PORT OF LONDON HAS
JUST BEEN SIGHTED AND THE MOOD IS CELEBRATORY.

BIG NOSE! - ACT FOUR

THE MOTHER COUNTRY

ALL	*IN THE MOTHER COUNTRY,*
HUBERT	*PLENTY FOR ALL TO SHARE*
ALL	*IN THE MOTHER COUNTRY,*
CLOVIS	*YOU'LL END UP A MILLIONAIRE*
ALL	*THE CRADLE OF DEMOCRACY;*
	THE HOME OF HOSPITALITY;
	IT'S THE PLACE FOR YOU AND ME,
	THE MOTHER COUNTRY.
HUBERT	*THOSE FRIENDLY FACES, THOSE HAPPY SMILES*
	WILL WELCOME ALL FROM CARIBBEAN ISLES,
CLOVIS	*THE ENGLISH FOLK WILL BE COMIN' OUT TO SAY*
	COME AND JOIN US BOYS, AND ENJOY YOUR STAY
PETER	*THE QUEEN WILL INVITE YOU AND ME*
	TO BUCKINGHAM PALACE FOR A GARDEN PARTY
ANOTHER	*AT THE HOME OF CRICKET, THE M.C.C.*
	WE'LL BE WELCOME THERE FOR CRUMPETS AND TEA
ALL	*IN THE MOTHER COUNTRY,*
HUBERT	*PAVEMENTS MADE OF GOLD*
ALL	*IN THE MOTHER COUNTRY,*
PETER	*IS IT ALWAYS SO DAMN COLD ?*
ALL	*THE CRADLE OF DEMOCRACY*
	THE HOME OF HOSPITALITY
	IT'S THE PLACE FOR YOU AND ME,
	THE MOTHER COUNTRY
ANOTHER	*THERE'S JOBS FOR A HARD WORKIN' BLOKE*
	JUST LOOK AT THOSE CHIMNEYS AND ALL THAT SMOKE
CLOVIS	*THERE MAY BE A LACK OF BRIGHT SUNSHINE*
	BUT I'VE SEEN ENOUGH TO LAST ME A LIFETIME
HUBERT	*I'M GOIN' TO EARN SO MUCH DOUGH*
	I'LL BE BACK WITH MY ROSEMARY IN SIX MONTHS OR SO
PETER	*THE TEMPERATURE'S MINIMAL AND THAT'S WHERE IT HURTS*
	I'M WEARING TWO JUMPERS AND ALL MI SHIRTS
ALL	*IN THE MOTHER COUNTRY,*
CLOVIS	*A WONDERFUL PLACE*
ALL	*IN THE MOTHER COUNTRY,*
PETER	*HAS ANYONE SEEN MI CASE?*
ALL	*THE CRADLE OF DEMOCRACY*
	THE HOME OF HOSPITALITY
	IT'S THE PLACE FOR YOU AND ME,
	THE MOTHER COUNTRY

BIG NOSE! - ACT FOUR

ACT FOUR - SCENE TWO

LONDON, SIX MONTHS LATER. EVENING

A DELAPIDATED TENEMENT IN LADBROKE GROVE. WE SEE THE ENTRANCE TO THE HOUSE, A FLIGHT OF STEPS LEADING UP TO THE FRONT DOOR AND THE INSIDE OF THE HOUSE.

THE BOYS ROOM IS ON THE FIRST FLOOR, VERY SPARSELY AND SHABBILY FURNISHED. WE CAN ALSO SEE THE LANDING AND STAIRS, WHERE THERE IS A SINK, AND THE TOILET, WHICH IS SIDE ON TO THE AUDIENCE ALLOWING US TO SEE THE OCCUPANT WHEN REQUIRED.

WHEN LIGHTS COME UP WE SEE CLOVIS ALONE IN THE ROOM AT THE TABLE WRITING. PETER LIES ON THE BED READING A NEWSPAPER.

CLOVIS AND HUBERT MET PETER ON THE BOAT TO ENGLAND, AND VINCENT, THE ORIGINAL TENANT OF THE ROOM, WHEN THEY LANDED. PETER AND VINCENT ARE COUSINS.

ENTER VINCENT

VINCENT   Boy, this country cold. Clovis, put on the kettle now man.

CLOVIS   You don't see I doin' somethin'. Your lazy cousin just lyin' there on the bed.

VINCENT   Peter, get up you lazy scamp. You look for a job today?

PETER   No.

VINCENT   Why not?

PETER   Cos I looked yesterday, and the day before that, and the day before that. And they told me the same thing: 'Sorry, mate we ain't got nothing for ya'

VINCENT   Yeah? Well, today might have been the day when he did have something for ya. You tink it was easy when I first get here to.....

PETER   Yeah, yeah, yeah. You nag like a woman.

    HE GETS UP TO PUT THE KETTLE ON AND GIVES THE NEWSPAPER TO VINCENT.

VINCENT   Boy, you can't talk about woman like dat in England you know.

BIG NOSE! - ACT FOUR

PETER   Woman? I don't see nothin' in England, all dem have is flat backside. I longin' to see a nice..big.. round......

CLOVIS   Shut up your mouth and make the tea.

VINCENT   What you doin', Clovis?

CLOVIS   Writin' home.

VINCENT   I hope you're lyin'.

PETER   Yes, tell 'em the sun is shinin', you got plenty money and you're livin' in a mansion, with a couple of good lookin' boys!

CLOVIS   Yes, there lays the lie.

               THE DOOR OPENS AND IN STEPS HUBERT

HUBERT   Boy how's this country so damn cold ?

               CLOVIS QUICKLY SCOOPS THE LETTER INTO HIS JACKET

VINCENT   You find a job boy?

HUBERT   No, but I hear they taking on plenty people tomorrow, down at the railway at Plaistow, we got to be there by eight o'clock.

PETER   But dat's miles away.

HUBERT   Anybody here didn't travel 4,000 miles to get a job?

PETER   Plaistow! Dat's a stupid idea.

HUBERT   Listen,I want a job. Who in here don't want a job ?

               PETER PUTS UP HIS HAND

PETER   Me. I want to go home. Dis place too damn unfriendly. Yesterday I was sittin' on the bus and this old Englishman spit on the floor right next to me. I mean what kind of manners is dat ?

               PETER GETS UP AND PUTS A KETTLE TO BOIL ON A GAS RING IN THE CORNER OF THE ROOM. HE MAKES HIS WAY TOWARDS THE CUPBOARD.

HUBERT   Why are White people so different here ?

CLOVIS   Back home we're used to the bosses, these are the workers.

HUBERT   What's for dinner?

BIG NOSE! - ACT FOUR

PETER What d'you think ?

        HE PICKS UP A SAD LOOKING STRING OF SAUSAGES AND SWINGS THEM TO AND FRO.

        Roast chicken, fried plantain with green banana and bloggo.

HUBERT Not sausages again, man.

PETER Vincent, can't you go and work in a chicken factory ?

VINCENT When all you get a job and can afford to bring in shoppin' we'll eat somethin' else.

        PETER PREPARES TO FRY THE SAUSAGES ON THE GAS RING.

PETER The kettle's boilin' pass me the milk. You know you're the only one who can open that stupid window.

        CLOVIS GOES TO THE WINDOW OPENS IT WITH DIFFICULTY AND TAKES THE MILK OFF THE SILL. CLOSES WINDOW. HE FEELS THE MILK IT'S COLD.

CLOVIS Better than a refridgerator. You want the butter? And have a lambi as well ?

PETER Ugh! How do you people eat that ?

HUBERT What you talkin' about its from the sea int'it.

VINCENT That thing look disgustin' to me.

HUBERT What you talkin' about that's a delicacy man. Anyway you can talk. You lot does eat monkey.

PETER [Who tell you dat ?
VINCENT [Dat's rubbish !

HUBERT My grandmother tell me dat people from your island does eat monkey, and you does fry it with coconut oil.

PETER Listen, at least we don't put sugar in our corn meal.

HUBERT Corn meal ? (TO CLOVIS) What is dat !

CLOVIS You know, what we call cuckoo.

PETER The thing is cornmeal, not no cuckoo !

CLOVIS I must tell you, this arguement is stupidness. Who call what food dis and dat !

BIG NOSE! - ACT FOUR

               THERE IS A KNOCK AT THE DOOR. IT OPENS.
               ENTER PHILPOT, A RACKMANESQUE LANDLORD AND HIS
               CHIEF RENT COLLECTOR MATHEW.

PHILPOT   'Allo boys ! Little domestic arguement. Keep it down, keep it down. Other residents here. (LAUGHING) Then I suppose it must be really difficult for you lot. Where you come from its kinda wild and noisy.

               SILENCE DESCENDS.

VINCENT   Good mornin' Mr. Philpot

PHILPOT   'Allo Vince. How's your job goin'?

VINCENT   Oh, fine, sir. In fact I'm just gettin' ready to go now.

PHILPOT   Good, good. You all know Mathew don't you ? Let me introduce you Matt. This is Vince and that's Cuthbert, Peter and the one with the big hooter is Hovis.

CLOVIS   My name is <u>Cl</u>ovis.

PHILPOT   Well, you all look the same, don't you. How do the lions tell you apart ?(LAUGHS)

               VINCENT AND PETER SMILE FEEBLY. CLOVIS SUCKS THIS TEETH.

PHILPOT   Well, enough of this idle chit chat. How long are you other boys planning to stay here ?

VINCENT   Well, Mr. Philpot, they're just lookin' for jobs now and as soon as they get one, they'll be leavin'.

PHILPOT   You know this is a room for two, but I'm willing to bend over backwards here: I'll allow you boys to stay, but I've got to put the rent up.

CLOVIS   What!

PHILPOT   Sorry boys, my hands are tied I'm getting complaints from the other residents, they can't get to the sink, there's guitar playing at four o'clock in the mornin'...

MATHEW   It's 35 shilling from now on.

BIG NOSE! - ACT FOUR

PHILPOT   He'll collect it on a wednesday.

VINCENT   But Mr. Philpot, none of the boys are workin'.

CLOVIS   This is outrageous. How are we goin' to be able to pay that ?

PHILPOT   Get yourself a job.

CLOVIS   What job! You think we're not lookin' for jobs everyday ?

PHILPOT   There's plenty of good jobs out there.

CLOVIS   What! Like the one your monkey's doin'!

MATHEW   Who you calling a monkey ?

CLOVIS   You ! What kind of man are you, doin' the white man's dirty work ?

PHILPOT   Come on now. What's colour got to do with it ? Its all this racialism that brings the world down.

CLOVIS   (TO MATHEW) It's people like you make me sick.

MATHEW   You wanna take this outside ?

CLOVIS   It'll be my pleasure. I'll whup you in the street like a dog !

THEY MOVE TOWARDS EACH OTHER. PHILPOT INTERVENES.

PHILPOT   Steady Mathew. Come on, stop this!

MATHEW STEPS BACK. PHILPOT PUTS HIS HAND ON CLOVIS' CHEST.

You need to calm down mate.

CLOVIS   Get your dirty, immoral, filthy hand off my clean shirt !

VINCENT   Clovis !

PHILPOT   You've got a big mouth, haven't you son.

CLOVIS   And you are a bloodsucker. How many poor West Indians are working their fingers to the bone to pay your extortionate rents for these despicable rooms ?

PHILPOT   If I were you I'd be careful mate.

CLOVIS   What can you do to me ? I'll beat you and your poodle.

BIG NOSE! - ACT FOUR

PHILPOT   Nobody's forcin' you to live here.

CLOVIS   Well I am ! And we're gonna pay the same rent we've been payin' for the last six months. I defy you to come and ask for more.

MATHEW   But you're not always gonna be here mate.

CLOVIS   Is that so ? Well from this moment on I will be the one opening the door. You'll meet me every time.

PHILPOT   There's more than one way to skin a cat. Let's go Mathew.

MATHEW   I'll see you wednesday.

                     PHILPOT AND MATHEW LEAVE

HUBERT   (CALLING AFTER THEM) Yes, you'll be collecting twenty-five shilling!

VINCENT   What the hell is wrong with you ? You want us to get kick out in the street ?

HUBERT   He was gonna kick us out anyway. Clovis was right, where we gonna get thirty-five shillin' from ?

PETER   But he didn't have to talk to him like that.

CLOVIS   So what was I gonna say: 'Please sir, oppress me some more.'

VINCENT   No, but you're supposed to talk to the man with decency, he's our landlord. After all, how many other white people lettin' us stay in their house ?

CLOVIS   So, that excuses him squeezing the blood out of us?

PETER   No, but it does mean that you should have some respect.

HUBERT   Respect ? How can you have respect for people like that ? I tell you Clovis, I was ready to whup them with you.

VINCENT   You see, I told you Peter, I told you when you wanted to bring those people into our house, that folk from those islands are ignorant.

HUBERT   What !

VINCENT   Dat's right, you're ignorant !

HUBERT   What do you know about my island ?

BIG NOSE! - ACT FOUR

VINCENT My daddy tell me never to mix with people like you, you violent and teef.

HUBERT You can talk. At least on my island we don't have to lock our door at night. You and your people lazy, you have no ambition. You let the white man walk all over you. You damn cowards!

PETER Who the rarse you callin' coward ?

HUBERT You !

THEY CONFRONT EACH OTHER. CLOVIS INTERCEDES.

CLOVIS Stop dis, stop dis. What the helld'you think you're doin'?

PETER You lot are too rude !

CLOVIS Listen, calm down. We are one !

PAUSE

You think when Teddy Boy see us in the street they gonna argue the finer points of inter-island Nationalism. No, wether you're from the East or the West, they just see you as: 'Black Bastard'.

THIS COOLS DOWN THE ARGUEMENT FOR A MOMENT.

PAUSE

VINCENT That may be. But Clovis, you were wrong.

CLOVIS Alright, I apologise.

LONG PAUSE. CLOVIS PICKS UP HIS GUITAR.

We all were wrong. We came here too naively.
We came expecting
The warmth of home;
To be in the smiles of these cold, hard people.
Because we'd given so much,
We ignored the hush
Of friends when asked: 'How's England ?'
Boys, we were wrong,
Because we'll never be strong
In a land that is not our own.

HUBERT That's right. That's why I want to go back.

CLOVIS STARTS TO PLAY, THE TONE IS VERY REFLECTIVE TO START WITH BUT GATHERS MOMENTUM AS THE OTHER THREE JOIN IN.

BIG NOSE! - ACT FOUR

THE WEST INDIAN FEDERATION (Reprise)

CLOVIS	*PLENTY OIL IN TRINIDAD* *JAMAICAN BAUXITE NOT SO BAD* *FREEDOM MAKE THE PEOPLE GLAD* *ITS THE BEST CHANCE WE EVER HAD*
HUBERT	*MONSERRAT AND ANTIGUA,* *ST. KITTS !*
CLOVIS	*DOMINICA AND GRENADA,*
HUBERT	*NEVIS !*
HUBERT	*THE WEST INDIAN FEDERATION*
CLOVIS	*THE ONLY SOLUTION*
HUBERT	*THE WEST INDIAN FEDERATION*
CLOVIS	*IS A VIABLE CONSTITUTION*
BOTH	*THE WEST INDIAN FEDERATION* *TALKIN' 'BOUT THE BIRTH OF A NEW NATION*
CLOVIS	*SO, MY FRIEND, DON'T TAKE OFFENCE,* *SHIFT YOUR ARSE, GET OFF DAT FENCE* *LISTEN TO ME I'M TALKIN' SENSE* *THE CARIBBEAN NEED HER INDEPENDENCE.* *TAKE A LESSON FROM MAHATMA GHANDI* *BRITAIN LEAVIN' WOULD SURE BE HANDY*
ALL	*THE WEST INDIAN FEDERATION*
CLOVIS	*THE ONLY SOLUTION*
ALL	*THE WEST INDIAN FEDERATION*
CLOVIS	*IS A VIABLE CONSTITUTION*
ALL	*THE WEST INDIAN FEDERATION* *TALKIN' 'BOUT THE BIRTH OF A NEW NATION*

SONG ENDS

THE FOUR LAUGH LOUDLY AS THE LIGHTS FADE.

BIG NOSE! - ACT FOUR

ACT FOUR - SCENE THREE

THE TENEMENT TWO DAYS LATER. NIGHT.

CLOVIS WALKS UP TO THE FRONT DOOR AS A BOTTLE CRASHES INTO THE STEPS BESIDE HIM. VOICES OFF FROM THE DIRECTION OF THE BOTTLE:

VOICE 1   We'll get you, you black bastard !

VOICE 2   Oi Sambo go back where you came from!

VOICE 3   Come on nig-nog !

HE ENTERS THE HOUSE. WALKS UP THE STAIRS TO THE ROOM. IN THE ROOM, HUBERT IS ASLEEP ON THE FLOOR. NEXT TO HIM LIES PETER AND, SNORING ON THE BED, VINCENT.

CLOVIS ENTERS THE ROOM CAREFULLY, STEPPING OVER THE SLEEPING PAIR.

CLOVIS PICKS UP HIS GUITAR AND RETRACES HIS STEPS. HE LEAVES THE ROOM AND HEADS FOR THE TOILET WHERE HE TAKES OUT PEN, PAPER AND ENVELOPE FROM HIS JACKET POCKET AND PUTS THE FINISHING TOUCHES TO A SONG.

BIG NOSE! - ACT FOUR

HOMESICK CALYPSO

CLOVIS
*HOME, THAT'S WHERE MY HEART LIES,
HOME, IN THIS COUNTRY I COULD NEVER DIE
HOME, WALK THE STREETS WITHOUT A CARE
AS LONG AS I HAVE BREATH LEFT IN ME
I SWEAR I'LL GET BACK THERE*

*OH, HOW I MISS THAT MORNIN' SEA BREEZE
LEMON GRASS AND THE TASTE IT LEAVES
MANGO JUICE, BOY, CAN'T GET ENOUGH,
DRINK SOME FISH BROTH MAKE YOUR BELLY BUFF.
COCONUT WATER, THEN DIVE IN THE SEA,
DRY OUT IN THE SUN, THEN KILL A ROTI.
LIME EVENIN' TIME WHERE THE THREE BANDS PLAY
SMILE TO MYSELF, THAT GO BE ME ONE DAY.*

*THAT'S WHY
HOME, THAT'S WHERE MY HEART LIES
HOME, IN THIS COUNTRY I COULD NEVER DIE
HOME, WALK THE STREETS WITHOUT A CARE
AS LONG AS I HAVE BREATH LEFT IN ME
I SWEAR I'LL GET BACK THERE.
AS LONG AS I HAVE BREATH LEFT IN ME
I SWEAR I'LL GET BACK THERE.*

SONG ENDS

BIG NOSE! - ACT FOUR

                A WOMAN TENANT, CELIA, ENTERS AND KNOCKS ON THE DOOR OF THE TOILET.

CELIA   What you doin' in there ?

CLOVIS   Erm.....erm...

                HE PUTS THE SONG IN THE ENVELOPE, SEALS IT AND PUTS IT BACK IN HIS JACKET POCKET.

CELIA   You want to wake up me children.

CLOVIS   Sorry, sorry. I comin' I comin'.

                CLOVIS FLUSHES THE TOILET AND OPENS THE DOOR. CELIA CLOCKS THE GUITAR.

CELIA   You think that its the Lyceum in there ?

                SHE WATCHES HIM RETURN TO HIS ROOM THEN GOES BACK INTO HERS.

                BACK IN THE ROOM CLOVIS GETS INTO BED WITH VINCENT.

VINCENT   Boy, where you comin' from this hour of the night?

CLOVIS   Nowhere.

VINCENT   Clovis, don't be a fool. Every night you do the same thing: creep out of bed, leave the house, creep back in an hour later. Where you does go ?

CLOVIS   I said nowhere. Go back to sleep. You'll wake up the others.

VINCENT   You have a little woman ?

CLOVIS   I tell you mind your business and go back to sleep.

VINCENT   When them Teddy Boy's kill your arse, that go be my business.

CLOVIS   Dem, you crazy, they can't catch me, boy.

VINCENT   Crazy. Dat's exactly what I was goin' to talk to you about. Why are you sitting in the toilet singing Calypso to yourself all night ? You think I'm not watching you ?

CLOVIS   Boy, don't let me have to tell you again, go to sleep.

VINCENT   Listen, it's my name on the rent book. It's me they comin' to when you disturb the whole house.

BIG NOSE! - ACT FOUR

CLOVIS IS CONCERNED ABOUT WAKING HUBERT.

CLOVIS If I tell you will you shut your mouth and go back to sleep.

VINCENT NODS.

I promised Hubert's wife, he'd write to her everyday. But look at him: the boy so cold he can hardly talk, let alone write. So, I do it.

VINCENT Boy, people from your island does do stupidness.

KISSES HIS TEETH TURNS OVER AND GOES BACK TO SLEEP

PAUSE

THERE IS A LOUD KNOCK AT THE DOOR.

VINCENT Who the hell's that!

CLOVIS Maybe our friend, the rent collector.

VINCENT (HUSHED) Peter, Hubert

A LOUDER KNOCK.

PETER What's up?

VINCENT Trouble.

VINCENT INDICATES THE DOOR AND SIGNALS TO THEM TO BE READY. HUBERT PICKS UP A CHAIR. CAREFULLY, CLOVIS OPENS THE DOOR TO REVEAL ROSEMARY. SHE IS CARRYING TWO LARGE SUITCASES.

ROSEMARY Hello Clovis.

CLOVIS Oh, my god, Rosemary !

HUBERT Rosemary ?

PETER TURNS ON THE LIGHT.

ROSEMARY Well this is a fine welcome.

HUBERT PUTS DOWN THE CHAIR. HE RUNS TO THE DOOR AND HUGS HER. THEN SUDDENLY WITHDRAWS AWARE OF THE SQUALOR OF THE ROOM AND THEIR NIGHTIME ATIRE.

HUBERT What are you doin' here ?

ROSEMARY Your letters drew me, no called me, to you. I was bombarded by lyrics so sweet, that my heart could not be apart from you a moment longer. Call it temporary madness, or the fever of love but I had to come. Arn't you gonna invite me in ?

BIG NOSE! - ACT FOUR

VINCENT   Clovis, where's your manners, invite the lady in.

                CLOVIS PICKS UP THE CASES. ROSEMARY STEPS IN. THE
                DOOR IS CLOSED. HUBERT WANDERS TO THE WINDOW.

CLOVIS   But how did you get here ?

ROSEMARY   By plane. What an adventure !

                SHE SITS ON THE BED

                First, I flew to Trindad on a tiny little thing,
                then I got on this huge one. Man, the airline
                people were so nice to me, well until I got to
                Heathrow. They've had me in customs half the night.

HUBERT   [What ?
CLOVIS   [What ?

PETER   This woman has the whole of her island in these
                bags !

                ROSEMARY MOVES TOWARDS THE CASES

ROSEMARY   Well, you see, after hearing about your delicious
                English diet, I decided you were in need of some
                home food !

                SHE OPENS THE SUITCASES TO REVEAL A FEAST OF
                CARIBBEAN CUISINE. THE MEN CHEER.

PETER   [O lord, O lord !
VINCENT   [Thank god.

                THEY RACE TOWARDS THE CASES.

CLOVIS   (IN JEST) Back off, this is small island food !

VINCENT   No, no, no, no, no we're all one you know !

                LAUGHING CLOVIS JOINS PETER AND VINCENT,
                INVESTIGATING THE CONTENTS OF ROSEMARY'S BAGGAGE.
                SMELLING AND SAVOURING THE DELIGHTS WITHIN.

ROSEMARY   Don't just stand there, get that pan on the stove!

PETER   No sooner said than done.

                PETER AND VINCENT START TO PREPARE THE FOOD. CLOVIS
                PICKS UP HIS GUITAR.

CLOVIS   Hey Hubert, look how they runnin' to eat the small
                island food now.

BIG NOSE! - ACT FOUR

IN PRAISE OF DUMPLIN'(Reprise)

CLOVIS
DUMPLING! HOW WE LOVE WE DUMPLING,
DUMPLING! HOW WE LOVE WE DUMPLING,

ROSEMARY
WHEN YOUR BELLY PLEADIN'
THERE'S SOMETHING THAT IT'S NEEDIN'
YOU KNOW WHERE YOUR BELLY SHOULD LEAD YOU
DON'T NEED A DIPLOMA,
JUST FOLLOW THE AROMA
THIS IS WHERE ROSEMARY GO FEED YOU.
FORGET ABOUT SAUSAGE AND BACON,
IF YOU'RE A BAJAN OR YOU'RE A JAMAICAN:

ANOTHER KNOCK AT THE DOOR. THE MUSIC AND SMELL OF COOKING FOOD HAS ATTRACTED THE OTHER TENANTS WHO START TO JOIN THE PARTY. HUBERT REMAINS ALOOF.

ROSEMARY
Come in, come in.

SHE HELPS VINCENT DISH OUT THE FOOD.

Home food, eat home food.

ALL
DUMPLING! BOY THEY'RE REALLY SOMETHING
DUMPLING! LET ME TELL YOU ONE THING.

ROSEMARY
YOU CAN FRY IT, YOU CAN BOIL IT,
YOU CAN BAKE IT, BUT YOU CAN'T FAKE IT.

CLOVIS PASSES THE GUITAR TO ONE OF THE TENANTS. MORE PEOPLE ARRIVE AND THE PARTY CONTINUES.

BIG NOSE! - ACT FOUR

CLOVIS APPROACHES HUBERT AT THE WINDOW.

CLOVIS There's something I've got to tell you. I wrote Rosemary some letters for you.

HUBERT So <u>you</u> asked her to come.

CLOVIS No. It's just that I promised her you would write.

HUBERT What?

CLOVIS Just one or two.

HUBERT How many letters did you write ?

CLOVIS Two. (PAUSE) Every day.

HUBERT You're crazy.

CLOVIS Careful she's coming over. This is the latest, it will help everything make sense.

ROSEMARY CROSSES TO THEM. CLOVIS MOVES AWAY AND LEAVES THE ROOM. THE PARTY CONTINUES

ROSEMARY What's wrong, my love ?

HUBERT You.

ROSEMARY Arn't you pleased to see me ?

HUBERT No, I'm not. I mean, of course I am. You weren't supposed to see me like this.

ROSEMARY Why, because you lied in your letter and said you were living in a mansion ?

HUBERT I.....

ROSEMARY I don't care if you're living in one room with three men. You are my husband and where you are, so should I be.

HUBERT You're planning to stay ?

ROSEMARY Yes. I'm here to be with you.

HUBERT But, you can't, you can't stay here. Where will you sleep ?

ROSEMARY Wherever you sleep my love. You said so in your last letter: 'Wherever I lay my head to rest, you are there'. Have you forgotten ? Of course you have you've written so many beautiful, sensual, emotional letters filled with elegant poetry. How could you remember every line ?

BIG NOSE! - ACT FOUR

HUBERT   I....

ROSEMARY   Yes, I know you love me.

            SHE KISSES HIM

            I've read, and re-read your letters, overjoyed in
            the knowledge that you have found me. The honesty..

HUBERT   That came over did it ?

ROSEMARY   You don't understand your own genius. I chastised
            myself for loving you, at first, for your external
            beauty; but now I know that your outward appearance
            is ugly in comparison to the beauty of your soul.

HUBERT   So now, it's my words that you're in love with.

ROSEMARY   Yes. Not trivial things, like your eyes, or your
            hair, the shape of your mouth, but the real you.

HUBERT   So, the words have taken you there.

ROSEMARY   Yes.

HUBERT   So even if I was ugly..?

ROSEMARY   ..even if your face was all askew I would still
            love you. In fact I want you to be ugly, because
            then you'll know how true my love is.

            SHE SEES THE LETTER IN HIS HAND. TAKES IT FROM HIM
            AND PUTS IT CLOSE TO HER HEART.

            You see, this is why I came.

            SHE KISSES HIM.

            VINCENT IS FRYING PLANTAIN. PETER IS WATCHING THE
            PAN. VINCENT IS WATCHING THE COUPLE

PETER   Ah, look at dat, isn't dat lovely.

VINCENT   When big man and woman kissing, look the other way.

            HE SLAPS PETER.

PETER   Ow!

HUBERT   I...I must find Clovis.

            PETER CROSSES TO ROSEMARY

            (COUGHS) As no one have the manners to introduce
            me, my name is Peter.

VINCENT   (MOUTH FULL OF FOOD) And I'm Vincent.

BIG NOSE! - ACT FOUR

ROSEMARY   ...Rosemary Lafayette. Pleased to meet you.

VINCENT   Come and get your food.

PETER   Quiet, quiet, quiet. I just want to say, if Hubert ever divorce this woman, I will gladly marry her. I love you Rosemary, my belly loves you Rosemary, thankyou for the food, Hip, hip...

ALL   Hooray!

SOMEONE ELSE PICKS UP THE GUITAR. PETER DANCES WITH ROSEMARY AS THE PARTY CONTINUES.

HUBERT FINDS CLOVIS ON THE STAIRS.

HUBERT   I need to talk to you, mister. This was all a scam for you, wasn't it? You love her !

CLOVIS   Hubert, stop. You love her, and she loves you.

HUBERT   What are you talking about ? She's in love with your words.

CLOVIS   Rubbish.

HUBERT   Why don't you just tell her?

HUBERT SHAKES CLOVIS.

HUBERT   The least you can be is honest. You love her !

PAUSE

CLOVIS   I do.

HUBERT   Then tell her.

CLOVIS   Don't be stupid.

HUBERT   Why is that being stupid ?

CLOVIS   Hubert, look at me.

HUBERT   Yes, you're grotesque. Your nose is big fat and ugly. But ugliness is what she wants; she just said she wants me to be ugly.

CLOVIS   Don't believe her, they're just words. And we know how they deceive, don't we ?

HUBERT   That's what our marriage was: a deception, a fraud.

BIG NOSE! - ACT FOUR

CLOVIS   No it wasn't, she loves you.

HUBERT   No, she's in love with your soul ! As stupid as I am, I need someone to love me for me, not who they want me to be.

                PAUSE.

                ROSEMARY COMES DOWN THE STAIRS. HUBERT SEES HER.

HUBERT   Clovis has something to tell you.

                HE RUSHES PAST HER RE-ENTERING THE ROOM. THE PARTY IS NOW VERY LOUD. CLOVIS WANDERS OUT OF THE HOUSE ONTO THE STEPS.

ROSEMARY   I seem to have vexed him. Is he alright, Clovis?

CLOVIS   Did you mean what you said to him?

ROSEMARY   What did I say?

CLOVIS   Even if he was ugly, grotesque...

ROSEMARY   Yes.

CLOVIS   ..twisted and deformed..

ROSEMARY   ...his soul would still be beautiful.

CLOVIS   You would still love him?

ROSEMARY   I would love him even more.

CLOVIS   (TO HIMSELF) Is it really possible? (TO HER) Rosemary......

                THE SOUND OF BREAKING GLASS, FOLLOWED BY THE WHOOSH OF A PETROL BOMB. SCREAMS AND SHOUTS THE MUSIC STOPS. FOR A MOMENT CLOVIS DOES NOT REGISTER THIS.

ROSEMARY   What was that?

CLOVIS   I've something I must tell you......

                A WHITE YOUTH RUNS ONSTAGE. SEEING ROSEMARY AND CLOVIS HE STOPS IN HIS TRACKS.

                What do you want, boy?

                FOR A MOMENT THEY STARE AT EACH OTHER.

TEDDY BOY   You bastards are gonna burn!

BIG NOSE! - ACT FOUR

>THEN, TERRIFIED THE YOUTH RUNS OFF IN ANOTHER
>DIRECTION. THE SOUND OF ANOTHER WINDOW AND PETROL
>BOMB.
>
>THE INHABITANTS OF THE TENEMENT COME STREAMING OUT
>OF THE HOUSE. SMOKE BEGINS TO CLOG THE STAIRCASE
>PETER STUMBLES OUT COUGHING.

ROSEMARY: Hubert, where's Hubert!?

PETER: He's right behind me.

>ROSEMARY SEARCHES FOR HUBERT. VINCENT STRUGGLES
>OUT, HE SUPPORTS HIMSELF ON CLOVIS.

VINCENT: We tried to put out the fire. Hubert wouldn't come. He's still in there, fighting it.

>CLOVIS ATTEMPTS TO GET BACK INTO THE HOUSE. THERE
>ARE STILL PEOPLE COMING OUT WHICH DELAY HIM.
>FINALLY HE MANAGES TO GET BACK IN. DENSE SMOKE IS
>NOW CLOGGING THE DOORWAY. WE LOSE SIGHT OF HIM.
>THE FLAMES INCREASE.
>
>HIGH ABOVE WE SEE THE SILHOUETTE OF HUBERT UP
>AGAINST A WINDOW AS THE FLAMES BURN BEHIND HIM.

ROSEMARY: (SCREAMING) Hubert!

>LIGHTS FADE TO BLACK AS THE NOISE OF THE FIRE
>INCREASES.
>
>AN INSTRUMENTAL OF 'HOMESICK CALYPSO' TAKES US INTO
>THE SCENE CHANGE.

END OF ACT IV

BIG NOSE! - ACT FIVE

ACT FIVE

THE ISLAND, TWENTY-FOUR YEARS LATER. FRIDAY, LATE
AFTERNOON. SUNNY, A COOL BREEZE BLOWS.

A PARK. CENTRE STAGE IS A LARGE MANGO TREE WITH
A CIRULAR BENCH BENEATH IT.

AS PEOPLE PASS THROUGH THE PARK A MALE NURSE PUSHES
AN ELDERLY SLEEPING PATIENT ONTO THE STAGE IN A
WHEELCHAIR AND PARKS HIM UNDER THE TREE. THE
PATIENT WEARS DARK GLASSES AND A PANAMA HAT. HIS
LEGS ARE COVERED WITH A BLANKET.

DEREK, THE NURSE, SITS DOWN ON THE BENCH WITH A
RADIO. HE TURNS ON THE RADIO. IT IS HIS FAVORITE
TRACK.

RADIO VOICE   *BING BONG JINGA JINGA DING DING*
              JUMP UP LET ME HEAR YOU SING
              BING BONG JINGA JINGA DING DING
              JUMP UP LET ME HEAR YOU SING

DEREK   Yeah boy! This a de boum!

HE JOINS IN THE SINGING AND DANCES AROUND. THE
ELDERLY PATIENT SLEEPS ON.

A FEMALE NURSE PUSHING ANOTHER SLEEPING PATIENT
ARRIVES ON THE SCENE.

DEREK   Paula ! Hey girl come make we jump up na ?

PAULA   Boy, stop your stupidness you don't see we are with
we patients ?

DEREK   Dem old people, dey dead to the world, man. Come
on.

SHE LOOKS AT HER SLEEPING CHARGE

PAULA   You're right.

SHE STARTS TO JOIN IN

BOTH   *BING BONG JINGA JINGA DING DING*
       JUMP UP LET ME HEAR YOU SING
       BING BONG JINGA JINGA DING DING
       JUMP UP LET ME HEAR YOU SING

BIG NOSE! - ACT FIVE

> ROSEMARY ENTERS ASSISTING A THIRD PATIENT LORD
> SUGARCOAT, WHO WALKS WITH THE AID OF A STICK. NOW A
> MAN IN HIS SIXTIES, HE CONTINUES TO WEAR HIS
> TRADEMARK HAT MADE OF SUGAR CANE. ROSEMARY, STILL
> AN ATTRACTIVE WOMAN, IS NOW IN HER EARLY FORTIES.
> SHE WEARS THE UNIFORM OF A SENIOR NURSE.

SUGARCOAT   You hear the stupidness these young people
            listening to today ? *JINGA JINGA BING BING !*

            PAULA SPOTS ROSEMARY

PAULA   Oh, Mrs. Lafayette, I was just takin' the patient
            back when.....

ROSEMARY   It's O.K. Off you go.

            PAULA WHEELS HER PATIENT FROM THE STAGE.

SUGARCOAT   Young man don't you feel ashamed, singing
            along with such stupidity ?

DEREK   No. Dat song is bad!

SUGARCOAT   Bad, bad, it's not bad it's terrible. Tell me what
            does 'Jinga, Jinga, Bing, Bong' mean ?

DEREK   I don't know. It don't have to mean anything, it
            just sound good.

SUGARCOAT   Sound good! Sound good! You young people today are
            corruptin' the grand inheritance, that the great
            calypsonians of the past bestowed upon you.

DEREK   Uh? Who are dey den?

SUGARCOAT   Who are dey! You mean to say you never heard of
            Jungle Lion, Genghis Khan, Clovis Dibiset: The Lord
            High Executioner and the greatest of them all:
            Lord Sugarcoat ?

DEREK   No.

            ROSEMARY LAUGHS. SUGARCOAT TURNS TO HER.

SUGARCOAT   You see, calypso is dead.

            HE STARTS COUGHING

DEREK   Dat's right and Soca a carry the swing now.

ROSEMARY   Sugar, calm yourself, you're not goin' to do your
            angina any good by carrying on this way. Derek
            Thomas, you may not work for me now, but I trained
            you to care for the elderly not provoke them.
            Turn off dat radio, you'll wake your patient.

BIG NOSE! - ACT FIVE

> DEREK KISSES HIS TEETH. TURNS OFF THE RADIO, PICKS UP A NEWSPAPER FROM BEHIND HIS WHEELCHAIR AND SITS DOWN BEHIND THE TREE. ROSEMARY HELPS SUGARCOAT TO THE TREE AND SITS DOWN BESIDE HIM ON THE BENCH.

ROSEMARY   You all right now, Sugar.

SUGARCOAT   Yes, I'm alright, it just saddens my heart. But, I like that young boy's style, see how he had that young girl jumpin' up? Boy, young love. What I wouldn't give to be that age again.

ROSEMARY   It's not all fun and Carnival for the young people these days, you know. It's not like when we were growing up. Things are hard now.

SUGARCOAT   Things were hard then.

ROSEMARY   These days are different, there's no work.

SUGARCOAT   What work was here in the fifties? You think dem people did run off to England for fun?

> ROSEMARY REMEMBERS HUBERT. SUGARCOAT SEES HER REACTION.

    I'm sorry, Rosemary...

ROSEMARY   It don't matter.

> LONG PAUSE.

SUGARCOAT   You know I think you should've married again.

ROSEMARY   They'll never be another man in my life. Hubert's last letter will stay here, next to my heart, forever.

SUGARCOAT   There comes a time when we all have to let go. It's not right that a woman should live out her life without a man.

ROSEMARY   I have a good life. Nursing is my life. Looking after all you old people is enough to fill three lives, I can tell you.

SUGARCOAT   Yes, but it's not the same Rosemary. I mean, look at Clovis.

> DEREK'S PATIENT WAKES UP AND STARTS TO LISTEN TO THE CONVERSATION.

BIG NOSE! - ACT FIVE

SUGARCOAT   I've never seen that man with a woman and he is
            unhappy, he is sad. That man has travelled to every
            island in the Caribbean and look, he has nothing
            to show for it. What does he have ?

ROSEMARY   He has memories. Memories far greater than any of
            us who've lived out our lives on this island.

SUGARCOAT   I don't mean to be rude, but how does he get his
            pleasure?

ROSEMARY   His weekly newspaper. He critise the police,
            the government, in fact anybody who, in his words:
            'abuses power' or 'prevents the advancement of
            West Indians'.

SUGARCOAT   That's all well and good, but I still think its
            very sad. You seeing him this evening?

ROSEMARY   Yes, its friday isn't it? Six o'clock on the dot,
            he'll be here. We'll sit under this tree, I'll do
            my crocheting and he'll read me the contents of
            'The Executioner's List'.

            THE SLEEPING PATIENT REMOVES HIS SUNGLASSES

DU BOIS   And it is that same list that will be the death of
            him.

SUGARCOAT   Mr. Du Bois!? How are you keeping? I didn't realise
            that was you there.

DU BOIS   Of course you didn't Sugarcoat, you've always been
            stupid, you and your whole family. Look at you, a
            young boy like you relyin' on a walkin' stick. When
            I was your age I was still runnin' after young
            girls, eh Rosemary. But I ain't runnin' no more.

ROSEMARY   How is your convalesence goin', Ignatius ?

DU BOIS   That stupid private hospital. Fly me to the states,
            triple by-pass, them people don't know nothing. I
            asked if I could come and stay at yours, but they
            said you wouldn't let me, its only for poor folk.

SUGARCOAT   Well, not everybody there is poor, you know.

DU BOIS   Rosemary, how are you?

ROSEMARY   I'm fine Ignatius, thankyou.

DU BOIS   I know you care for the poor, but would you decline
            the request of a rich old man for a stroll round
            the park?

ROSEMARY   I'm here with Sugarcoat.

BIG NOSE! - ACT FIVE

DU BOIS   Derek, come and baby sit Sugarcoat.

                ROSEMARY PUSHES DU BOIS UPSTAGE. DEREK APPROACHES SUGARCOAT.

DEREK   Goo, goo ,googa. Come to daddy.

SUGARCOAT   Boy, watch it. Dat sound like one of dem Soca lyric.

                BASIE, NOW IN HIS FORTIES, RUNS ON OUT OF BREATH.

BASIE   Sugarcoat, Sugarcoat, where's Miss Rosemary?

SUGARCOAT   Why what you want?

BASIE   Someting terrible's happened, man.

                HE SITS DOWN

                Oh, my god dat never could've been no accident.

SUGARCOAT   What are you talkin' about!

BASIE   Our freind, Clovis. I was walkin' down Harbour Street when I saw Clovis crossin' the road. From out of nowhere I saw this truck reversin' as if it was goin' to hit him. All of a sudden, there's a screech of brakes, and all I can see is oil barrel fallin' out the back. Well one hit him in the foot and trow him off balance. The next one hit him in the head. Bam! He fall.

SUGARCOAT   What!

BASIE   It must be like six, seven, eight, nine rollin' at him.

SUGARCOAT   What kind of drivin' is dat?

BASIE   This is the ting: the driver never even stop to see what happen, the truck just drive off.

SUGARCOAT   So, what happen to Clovis?

BASIE   Well, he was just lyin there, with a big cut in his head. Man it was terrible the blood mixin' up with the oil. He wouldn't let us take him to the hospital.

SUGARCOAT   He dead?

BASIE   No, no, no, a few of us manage to drag him back to his house an I call the doctor.

BIG NOSE! - ACT FIVE

SUGARCOAT Oh my word. You musn't tell Rosemary, not yet. Let we go see him quick.

BASIE I got the car over here.

SUGARCOAT Soca Boy, tell Mrs. Lafayette I was cold and I had to go back and Basie's takin' me.

SUGARCOAT AND BASIE START TO LEAVE

And don't repeat a word of what you've just heard.

DEREK Bloody old people. You go soon dead!

HE SITS DOWN AGAIN. ROSEMARY AND DU BOIS RETURN.

DU BOIS So you've forgiven me?

ROSEMARY We're here right now, arn't we?

DU BOIS You must really have loved dat boy.

ROSEMARY He was everything a man should be.

DU BOIS I can't understand such devotion to someone who is dead.

ROSEMARY But he isn't dead. We still meet in a special place sustained by love - a living love.

DU BOIS How is....Clovis?

ROSEMARY Oh, he's well. Actually, he's not, sometimes I see him and he looks as though he hasn't eaten for three days. But he won't let me help him, he's a proud man.

DU BOIS He has made a lot of enemies. His newspaper attacks politicians, the church, prominant businessmen, y'know respectable people. I even heard the other day, that a huge deal with a foriegn investor may have fallen through, because of something he has printed.

ROSEMARY Clovis has always spoken his mind.

DU BOIS It's time that boy learn you can't just open your mouth about any and everything. It didn't do him no good in England did it. Or in any of the islands where he tried to drum up support for his Pan-Caribbean Black Unity whatever.

PAUSE

What time you expecting him?

BIG NOSE! - ACT FIVE

ROSEMARY   Six o'clock, he's never late.

DU BOIS   Somehow, though I have everything, and he has nothing, I envy him. He has lived his life with, dare I say, honour. Maybe one day I'll be man enough to tell him that. Derek, take me home.

ROSEMARY   Where is Sugarcoat ?

DEREK   He said for you not to worry, he's gone back.

DEREK PUSHES DU BOIS FROM THE STAGE. AS HE GOES. A NEARBY CHURCH CLOCK STRIKES SIX.

DU BOIS   I'll see you again?

ROSEMARY   Yes, you shall.

ROSEMARY SITS UNDER THE TREE AND TAKES OUT HER CROCHET WORK. SHE LOOKS AROUND FOR CLOVIS THEN RETURNS TO HER STITCHES.

AFTER A PAUSE CLOVIS ARRIVES CARRYING HIS GUITAR WALKING VERY SLOWLY. HE IS WEARING A HAT WHICH CONCEALS HIS BANDAGED HEAD.

CLOVIS   I'm sorry I'm late, someone detained me in the street.

SHE DOESN'T LOOK UP FROM HER WORK

ROSEMARY   An old aquaintance?

CLOVIS   Someone I've been avoiding for many years.

ROSEMARY   What did they want?

CLOVIS   I told them, 'This is friday, I have a regular appointment'. I said I'd see them in an hour or so.

ROSEMARY   They'll have to wait longer than that. We have the whole week to catch up on.

CLOVIS   Well, we'll see.

ROSEMARY   You're in a melancoly mood.

CLOVIS   Me, I'm not the melancoly type.

HE STRUMS A CHORD ON HIS GUITAR TO SHOW HIS MOOD.

Let me read something from 'The Executioner's List':

BIG NOSE! - ACT FIVE

CLOVIS
The first head to fall, I don't make no mistakes,
Is the President of the United Snakes.
What possible threat could our island be
To the Land of the Base, where Corruption flows
                                             Free?

This poor little island you want to ransack.
You threaten our leaders and warn of attack.
Forgotten the lessons you learnt in Vietnam,
That the spirited few can defeat Uncle Sam?

ROSEMARY
You don't think that's a bit strong ?

CLOVIS
Hell no, that's just for starters. Wait till you hear what I've written about our beloved Prime Minister:
You fat greedy pig, always stuffing your face,
Can't you see your behavior's disgracing the race?
You've raided our coffers for an untold amount,
You think we don't know 'bout that Swiss bank
                                        account?

Your wife walking round with her crocodile shoes
If she wear one pair twice, she say she abuse.
We know tax increases you're wanting to pass,
Strippin' the poor man, exposing his.....

AT THE END OF HIS POEM HIS HEAD DROPS LEAVING THE LAST LINE UNFINISHED.

ROSEMARY
Clovis!

CLOVIS
(WAKING UP) What? Yes, what, what?!

ROSEMARY
Are you alright ?

CLOVIS
Yes, I just have a little pain.

ROSEMARY
Well, we all have our pain to bare.

PUTS HER HAND ON HER HEART

CLOVIS
Hubert's last song to you. Didn't you promise me one day I could read that ?

ROSEMARY
Yes I did.

CLOVIS
Could I read it now.

ROSEMARY
Now ?

CLOVIS
Yes, today.

SHE WALKS OVER AND GIVES IT TO HIM.

ROSEMARY
You have my heart in your hands. Be careful, you're the only person I would trust with such a precious thing.

BIG NOSE! - ACT FIVE

SHE SITS BACK DOWN AND RESUMES HER WORK
CLOVIS BEGINS TO SING 'HOMESICK CALYPSO'

HOMESICK CALYPSO (Reprise)

CLOVIS
*HOME, THAT'S WHERE MY HEART LIES
HOME, IN THIS COUNTRY I COULD NEVER DIE
HOME, WALK THE STREETS WITHOUT A CARE
AS LONG AS I HAVE BREATH LEFT IN ME
I SWEAR I'LL GET BACK THERE.*

ROSEMARY
It's strange hearing a male voice recite those words....

CLOVIS
*BUT MOST OF ALL, THE CARIBBEAN SUN
LOOKS DOWN EACH DAY ON MY PRECIOUS ONE
WHILE I AM BLIND IN THIS DARK PLACE,
I DREAM OF HER HAND ON MY FACE.
A PRISONER WITH NO HOPE OF PAROLE
CHAINS ROUND MY BODY, CHAINS ROUND MY SOUL
ONLY ONE THING CAN SET ME FREE
A KISS FROM THE LIPS OF SWEET ROSEMARY.*

ROSEMARY
If the theme wasn't love, that song could be your own.

SHE TURNS TO SEE HIM

Clovis, you haven't opened the letter. How do you know the words ?

HE LOOKS UP GUILTY. THE REALITY DAWNS FOR ROSEMARY.

ROSEMARY
Oh, my god. Oh my god. It was you, you wrote all those letters.

CLOVIS
Rosemary.....

ROSEMARY
For twenty-four years you have pretended to be my friend, when really....

CLOVIS
No, Rosemary....

ROSEMARY
How stupid of me, I should have...

CLOVIS
Rosemary, I swear....

ROSEMARY
The Balcony Song!

CLOVIS
....on my life.....

ROSEMARY
It was you, it was all you.

CLOVIS
It wasn't me that loved you.

ROSEMARY
Yes it was !

BIG NOSE! - ACT FIVE

CLOVIS · No, it wasn't, it was Hubert.

ROSEMARY · Don't lie, look me in my eye and tell me that you never loved me !

CLOVIS · I never loved....

ROSEMARY · You love me. After all of these years, why would you break your silence now ?

BASIE RUNS ON, FOLLOWED CLOSELY BY SUGARCOAT.

BASIE · He's here! Thank god we've found him. Rosemary, the man needs hospital attention.

ROSEMARY · Clovis what's wrong?

CLOVIS · Please excuse me I didn't get to the end of my list.

Some teefs in this land I'm determined to foil;
They steal our resources, it makes my blood boil.
Degrading the ocean, pollutin' the soil,
Don't care what they kill for a barrel of oil.
The powers of evil, they now have decreed,
My breath must be stopped by the forces of greed.
The land can be taken, the poor pay more rent,
Now they have silenced the voice of dissent.

HE COLLAPSES

ROSEMARY · Clovis, what have they done to you?

CLOVIS · Rosemary, Rosemary.

ROSEMARY · I love you.

CLOVIS · To hear those words come from your lips, means I can die a happy man.

ROSEMARY · You have to live.

SUGARCOAT · You're not gonna die, Clovis.

ROSEMARY · How unhappy I must have made you.

CLOVIS · No, you have made me the happiest man alive, Because of you, I have known what it is to love. Without you I would never have known the sweetness of woman. You have loved me Rosemary, you have loved me twice.

ROSEMARY · You can't die my love, now you are my only love.

BIG NOSE! - ACT FIVE

CLOVIS   Sky above is blue,
              Sea is deep and green,
              None lovelier
              Than my Island Queen.

              CLOVIS DIES IN ROSEMARY'S ARMS.

              AS THE LIGHTS FADE ON THE FIGURES AROUND HIM
              BEHIND LIGHTS COME UP ON THE BAND WHO PLAY A
              REPRISE OF:

HOME SICK CALYPSO

HOME, THAT'S WHERE MY HEART LIES,
HOME, IN THIS COUNTRY I COULD NEVER DIE.
HOME, WALK THE STREETS WITHOUT A CARE
AS LONG AS I HAVE BREATH LEFT IN ME
I SWEAR I'LL GET BACK THERE.

END OF 'BIG NOSE'

Hold on... was first performed as *BLUES BROTHER SOUL SISTER* at The Bristol Old Vic Theatre 6th Feb 1999
The cast were as follows:

Rufus	Kwame Kwei-Armah
Orletta	Ruby Turner
Pepsi	Dawn Michael
Maylika	Paulette Ivory

And an on stage seven piece Soul Band

And Feb 2000

Rufus	Kwame Kwei-Armah
Orletta	Ruby Turner
Pepsi	Chardel Rhoden
Maylika	Pepsi Demacque
Julie	Llewella Gideon

And an on stage seven piece Soul Band

And on National tour Autumn 2001

Orletta	Ruby Turner
Rufus	Peter Straker
Julie	Jacqui Boatswain
Pepsi	Dawn Michael
Maylika	Veronica Hart

Covers
Orletta	Mary Pearce
Sisters	Bosede Are

And an on stage seven piece Soul Band

All productions directed by	Andy Hay
Musical direction on all productions	John O'Hara
Set Design	Mick Bearwish
Choreography by	Karen Bruce (99-2001)
	Dolly Henry (2000)
Lighting by	Tim Streader

ACT ONE

SCENE ONE

Lights up.

Three women, Orletta, Pepsi and Maylica are standing on stage each in their own 'inner' world. As if we are at three separate locations a 'special' spotlight separates each from the other. All the women are at a different emotional point in their lives. Maylika has just kicked her man out, Pepsi has just walked out of mothers home for good, and Orletta is just fed up with life. They sing the words to the song with those emotions in mind. Maylika sings the first verse. They all join in on the Chorus

PIECE OF MY HEART by Erma Franklin

*The song continues as lights come up on **Pepsi.***
She sings the second verse

Lights go down on Pepsi and rise on Orletta

Orletta sings the chorus.

When it has ended she stops, looks at the audience and says:

ORLETTA Ah bollocks to this.

The band play through to the end of the number lights down.

SCENE TWO

We are on the stage at the venue where the gig will be performed tonight.

*Lights up on **the band & Rufus** who are rehearsing. Rufus is singing the soul classic*

KNOCK ON WOOD

The song ends.
Rufus makes his way over to the piano, sits and starts to work on some vocal arrangements.
Enter Julie his manager. She stops and thinking for a moment about the best way to approach Rufus. She's got it. She walks over to the him at the piano, the personification sweetness

JULIE	Rufus? I've been hearing this song on the radio, and I kept thinking to myself' "that's a Rufus song".
RUFUS	(*Not really interested*) Yeah! What kinda style was it?
JULIE	'Morderny'
RUFUS	Moderny, what the hells morderny?
JULIE	I don't know how to describe it except it's kinda like what you hear on the radio everyday but it was really good
RUFUS	The music on the radio these days is bloody rubbish.
JULIE	Anyway I called up the publishers and they've just got back saying their interested in maybe hooking you and the songwriter up.
RUFUS	(*Suddenly interested*) Oh yeah?
JULIE	All they need is a tape of you (*She takes a deep breath*) singing something modern.
RUFUS	My voice don't sit down on no transcendental Ayibiza hip house music. No
JULIE	A good voice is a good voice no matter what's going on around it.
RUFUS	Julie. How many times we gonna have this conversation? I'm only gonna do what I'm good at. All they want singers to do these days is shout and scream and wear tops that show off their breast. And that's the men. I don't need fame and fortune that much
JULIE	You do!
RUFUS	All-right maybe I do. But those hungry days will soon be gone baby. For the last time I am the artist you're the manager.
JULIE	Maybe for the last time.
RUFUS	Sorry?
JULIE	I swear no one would believe you're a young man. I know some granddads with more swing than you
RUFUS	Don't worry about me baby, I got the swing where it counts

He mockingly attempts to pinch her bottom

RUFUS (*Winking*) Or have you forgotten?

JULIE (*Seriously*) Stop your stupidness

RUFUS Sorry.

Enter Steve the M.D. Rufus quickly turns to him

RUFUS Hey Steve, how were rehearsals this morning with the new girl?

STEVE Cooking Ruf!

RUFUS Cooking? Do I look like bloody Delia Smith? (*To Julie*) I asked the man how rehearsal went and he gives me some blasted hot out of the ghetto response. (*To Steve*) I live in Crouch End we don't talk like that there you know

STEVE (*Acquiescing*) It's been terrific thank you Rufus.

RUFUS Wicked rude boy. So this new girl, has she got a voice?

Out of sight of Rufus Julie is frantically trying to indicate to Steve not to talk about the new girl. He doesn't quite know what she trying to say

JULIE The best.

RUFUS Steve?

STEVE Yeah

RUFUS Good. Well tonight will be a bit bumpy but the big folk ain't coming in till tomorrow so we'll just have to live with it. Julie, how's all of that going by the way?

JULIE Great. I spoke to the PNO people this morning, they said they were all really looking forward to the gig.

RUFUS Yeah?

JULIE And I've been told confidentially that it's just out of you and another act . They've blown out all the others.

Rufus punches the air and dances with himself

RUFUS   Yes! Sixty G's a year, and cruising round the world.

JULIE   Lets not get too excited now, the gigs not in the bag yet.

RUFUS   Ah, have faith, I can taste it in my waters

She raises an eyebrow

RUFUS   You know what I'm trying to say.

JULIE   Right.

RUFUS   I can just see me now. Between gigs. Taking in the sun on the deck of the ship, watching all the ….

JULIE   ….Pensioners

RUFUS   Pretty young things walking by. And then I'll spot land. Mexico maybe, and I'll be

He goes into deep daydream land he begins to sing the Otis Redding Classic.

DOCK OF THE BAY

He sings unaccompanied at first. The band joining a few instruments at a time in later

The song ends

Snapping him out of his reverie Julie shouts

JULIE   Rufus. Rufus! Stop your stupidness.

RUFUS   (*Angry for being woken from his beautiful dream*) I don't know why I let you talk to me like that you know

JULIE   Maybe because I've washed your dirty underpants.

RUFUS   (*Rufus coughs wanting to move straight on*) What time are the girls due back?

JULIE   Oh shit! in about five minutes or so.

RUFUS   All right, where's my clothes?

JULIE   In your dressing room....along the corridor, second on the right, number two.

RUFUS   TWO?

JULIE   The sink in "one" was broken.

RUFUS   Oh right, Respect to that.

Rufus exits. Steve comes up to Julie.

STEVE   What was all that staring about?

JULIE   I forgot to tell you. He doesn't know who the new girl is.

STEVE   Oh my god

Enter Orletta from the opposite end of the stage that Rufus exited. She is isolated in a pool of light. Orletta sings her life statement. Julie will over hear the last line.

ORLETTA   *The thrill has gone*
          the thrill has gone away for good
          The thrill has gone baby
          the thrill has gone away
          Well you know that you done me wrong
          and one day you gonna pay

JULIE   Girl you still singing them old blues?

ORLETTA   Hey, if it ain't the blues it's the funk. You know I should combine the two, create my own sound, yeah blue funk. Ummm Funk blues, no Blue funk

She sings

ORLETTA   My man just leave me, so I bought my self a brand new bag. Help me good god.

She does a James Brown move. They laugh

JULIE   Girl you still crazy.

ORLETTA In this world if you ain't a little crazy you'll go mad. Know what I'm saying?

They touch hands

JULIE I hear you. Thanks for doing this Orletta,

ORLETTA It beats daytime TV and signing on.

JULIE Stop that loser bizness

ORLETTA Still managing your Ex is what I call loser bizness. Julie you're my mate and I love's ya, but what you still doing here? The man is a loser!

JULIE Steady, that's my artist you're talking about

ORLETTA You shoulda dropped that clown and taken your HALF years ago

JULIE Maybe I'm waiting for my half to be a little over 55 pence!

ORLETTA Alright!!!!! Now you're talking, I knew you were suffering for a reason.

JULIE I'm only kidding Orletta. I just want to set him up right….once I've done that I tell you….. I'll be….

ORLETTA You'll be what? Talk to me girl

JULIE I'll be gone. Off to Bali to write that novel, discover the next big internet something, just anything except what I'm doing right now. (*She kisses her teeth*) Anyway, enough of my stupidness

ORLETTA Girlllllllllll, you're forgetting who we are

They sing a bit from Bob Marleys Survivors

Na na na na na na
Were the survivors
The black survivors

They hug and Julie kisses her on the cheek

ORLETTA That's right, so lets get mission rescue Julie on the road.

JULIE (*Getting back to business*) Did you bring the music we talked about?

ORLETTA Hell yeah. Have you told Rufus yet that I'm his replacement……

JULIE No. I haven't quite worked out the best way to do that.

ORLETTA We'll be slipping from Smokey Robinson to Spice girls, before he bats an eye-lid.

JULIE Excellent. Show Steve some of the dot's before Rufus gets back?

ORLETTA Good Idea. Hey stixs!

She heads for her bag and then to Steve.

*Enter **Pepsi** and **Maylika**, they are in conversation*

PEPSI What's up people! Wha! Rude girl, last night I fell asleep working on my harmonies. But my man woke me up, gave me hot cup of mint tea, then helped me get the last song down pat.

MAYLIKA That's cute. We all need some one like that in our lives uh?

PEPSI Yeah man, but it's about how you train em you know. You got to be hard from the get go. Don't take no back chat, know what I'm saying?

MAYLIKA (*Smelling bull*) Yes, I know what you're saying.

Pepsi's mobile rings. Everybody on the stage pulls out their mobile. but we should focus ultimately on Maylika as she pulls out her mobile with much alacrity. She's expecting a call but alas it's for Pepsi

PEPSI YO!!!. …….Oh mum!!!!(*She's surprised and begins to slightly stutter*) Where am I? Em (*She moves away from Maylika and crunches up a bit of paper into the phones microphone*) I'm in traffic, I'll call you back. Bye.

She is nearly busted. She suddenly gets very hot so she fans herself to cool down. She exhales. When Julie hears Pepsi say 'mum' she looks over concerned.

In the meantime Maylika who has put on her headset and is rehearsing some of the moves spots Julie. She goes over to her.

MAYLIKA	Hi Julie! I just wanted to check with you that it is cash in hand directly after the gig right?
JULIE	(*She does not dig Maylika*) Who gave you that idea?
MAYLIKA	Em Rufus.
JULIE	When did he tell you that?
MAYLIKA	After rehearsals last night on the way to the pub
JULIE	Oh he did did he?
MAYLIKA	Yes. He said that I was to check that with you, but that was the impression he was under
JULIE	Well if Rufus says that it's cash in hand *directly* after the gig, then cash in hand it is.
MAYLIKA	Right. Thanks for that. You didn't mind me asking you did you?
JULIE	No. Of course not.
	She gives her a fake smile and Maylika goes back to her rehearsing
JULIE	I'm gonna kill that man.
	Julie walks over to Pepsi
JULIE	Are you ok?
PEPSI	Yeah I'm cool man.
JULIE	That was you're mum right?
	Pepsi nods her head
JULIE	I feel really bad getting you involved in this
PESPI	Oh don't. I'm cool wid it
JULIE	I must tell you I ain't sure about all this 'Pepsi street wise bizness', you're a pastors daughter how can you be carrying on like that?
PEPSI	Trust me, it's all part of my angle

JULIE   All right! You're doing great for your first time.

PEPSI   This is what I want to do Aunty Julie.

JULIE   Less of the Aunty if you please.

PEPSI   I can't help it. I was a kid watching you on the TV saying Bomshaka 'That's my aunty, and I'll be like her one day'

Julie smiles. Then whispers in her ear

JULIE   People on the street don't say Bomshaka any more!

PEPSI   Oh yeah?

JULIE   No. Listen if any of this gets too uncomfortable, just come and talk to me right!

PEPSI   I will

JULIE   Promise?

PEPSI   Yeahhhhh.

JULIE   Good. Oh, and the next time you call me Aunty I'll slap you up. I'm just about old enough to be your... em older sister. Bloody cheek

Pepsi laughs

Enter Rufus smoosing on the phone. He doesn't see Orletta at first.

RUFUS   .... Na I'm back in town honest. Soon soon believe. Listen come meet me after the show. I'll speak to you later. Ciao Bella.

ORLETTA Ciao bella. So you speak Italian now?

Rufus turns around and see Orletta. He is shocked

ORLETTA Hi Rufus.

RUFUS   What the hell are you doing here?

ORLETTA I'm your replacement girl. Isn't that great?

RUFUS	My replacement what!?
	He runs over to Julie is about to leave. She braces herself
RUFUS	Julie tell me I'm reaming or did I just imagined that Orletta Duplone is my replacement singer.
JULIE	She was the only person I could find that was available
RUFUS	The only person you could find? I don't believe you
JULIE	I'm sorry, but you sacked the other…
RUFUS	…Sorry!? You better do better than that. Get rid of her.
JULIE	Don't be stupid. I'm serious Rufus, she was the only person I could get that would step in at such short notice.
RUFUS	I don't care Julie. I can't work with her
JULIE	And I've already paid her
RUFUS	What!. (*He stops in his tracks*)
JULIE	Rufus. Be professional. Come on. Keep your eye on the prize. It's time to start the rehearsal; you're embarrassing yourself.
	He reluctantly walks back into the centre.
RUFUS	Ok every body lets focus. Rehearsals have been going well but I just want us to go to the next level today. This is a tribute to the male singing stars of the sixties. But unlike most tribute bands who just have to be faithful to one band, we have to be faithful to the music of a whole era. So our responsibility is to bring that era back to minds of our audience in absolute three D Technicolor. It ain't easy, but at the risk of sounding cocky, I've done it before. . I quote The Guardian, 'When Rufus walks on stage enter the Original Soul Man'. I'm sorry about the sacking of Susan but If you don't cut the slack you get the sack, know what I'm saying ya'll. Anyway witty Americanisms aside, are we ready to get busy
PEPSI	Yes Mr. Rufus
RUFUS	Just Rufus Pepsi, Mr Rufus is my dad

PEPSI	Yeah yeah yeah Cool!
RUFUS	OK, lets put some bollocks into this rehearsal

Rufus makes to start the rehearsal, but Orletta says

ORLETTA	Sorry Rufus could I just ask why this is a tribute to the *male* singing stars of the sixties?
RUFUS	Because I want it to be. Do you have a problem with that?
ORLETTA	Moei? Noooo. Sixties girl me

Orletta mimics a sixties dance move

RUFUS	So, can we pick up where we left off last night. That's the harmony section on Soul Man
ORLETTA	*(She sings to herself)* This is a man's mans world But it would mean nothing nothing He wouldn't be here with out a woman or a girl
MAYLIKA	Rufus, are the band staying with us till the show?
RUFUS	Hell yeah. And ain't they one funky set of white boys?

They smile. She is gently flirting, but most importantly letting Rufus know that she doesn't have a problem with his set. She is here to work and get paid

RUFUS	That's why our stuffs got to be right
MAYLIKA	That's really good, you don't get to work with the band before a gig a lot these days
RUFUS	Yeah? Well I like to do things the right way you know.

She retreats

He goes to the piano and plays the first chord

RUFUS	Alright girls. Here are you notes. 1 2 3 4

They start to sing the harmony

I'M A SOUL MAN
I'M A SOUL MAN

But Pepsi sings a horribly flat note

RUFUS What the hell was that! Pepsi let me listen to your line please

Horror descends onto Pepsi's face. To protect her Orletta takes the blame

ORLETTA No, it was me that went out, instead of singing *(she sings the wrong notes)* I sang *(she sings the right notes)*

RUFUS *(Not wholly convinced)* OK then, lets do it again 1 2 3

THEY DO.

ALL *I'M A SOUL MAN*
I'M A SOUL MAN

You can see the nervousness on Pepsi's face. Orletta winks at her. it's fine this time

RUFUS OK, but remember you gotta sing it like men. You're the three back up tops to my lead top.

GIRLS *(Look at each other confused)* RIGHT.

RUFUS Moving on. Lets go to the harmony section from 'What becomes of the broken hearted'

ORLETTA Now that's a woman's song. What do men know about broken hearts eh?

MAY I hear that!

Pepsi laughs. Rufus gets paranoid

RUFUS What do you mean by that?

ORLETTA *(Innocently)* Nothing

RUFUS Yes you did? What did that comment mean Orletta?

ORLETTA   It meant that women can relate to the words in that....

RUFUS   Ohh here we go again. Men are the only ones that break hearts right?

ORLETTA   Yep. Am I lying girls?

MAY   You sure ain't

Pepsi giggles in agreement

RUFUS   Oh and women are the only ones that hurt!!!

ORLETTA   That's not what I said, I simply said that women can relate to the the sentiments of that song

RUFUS   Well let me tell you something young lady, in my book, men are the only ones that truly love, but I don't bring that into the rehearsal room.

The women react with great doubt

ORLETTA   What?

He cuts in on her

RUFUS   If you want to carry on in this business I suggest you lose that chip on your shoulder. Do you get me?!!

Orletta is outraged

ORLETTA   What? Where the hell do you get off talking to me like that Rufus. If you remember correctly it was me who gave you your first gig in this business.

RUFUS   Yeah yeah yeah, but I'm the boss now.

ORLETTA   Let me tell you something

The lights change. We are not in real time but in the mind of Orletta. Rufus is oblivious to everything that is happening.

*She breaks into the seminal Aretha Franklin number **Think** bang on the verse*

THINK

ORLETTA   YOU BETTER THINK

The song ends. On the last beat Rufus who is at the Piano speaks. The girls are all stood around the piano as if they have just finished rehearsing a harmony line with Rufus

RUFUS   Shall we try it again!

At that point Julie enters.

JULIE   Rufus can I speak to you a minute please.

RUFUS   (*Aggressively*) I'm in the middle of rehearsal Julie!

JULIE   (*She bites her tongue*) I know, but I'll only take a minute

She stands back turned waiting in her little office area of the stage.

RUFUS   Alright guys take five. Yes my love?

She turns violently

JULIE   First of all don't talk to me like that in front of the artist….

RUFUS   Like what darling?…….

JULIE   What the hell is wrong with you, how could you tell Mayleeka whatever her name is, that we are going to pay her cash in hand after the gig. We haven't paid the last girls yet you want to go and run up your show off mouth and say……

RUFUS   Wo wo wo wo, steady girl. Look at her! That girl is talent. We are lucky to have her on board. I thought that she might be getting a little nervous and so to placate her I said that we would pay her after the gig what's the problem?

JULIE   The problem Mr smooth operator is that we ain't got no money to be paying her or anyone, until the management pay us. And you know for a fact, these suckers pay late. You want me to entertain the P n O people, pay the artist, pay the band…For goodness sake you let your willy rule your head.

RUFUS   That's really wrong. Why you gotta be bringing up the past all the time?

JULIE   Because it's always relevant to you Rufus. I am the one that they are going to come to, to ask for the money!

RUFUS   *(He loses it then steams off)* Well then you deal with it.

JULIE   Oh I will. What did I ever see in that man? Please God let him get this gig

RUFUS   Right girls! I really can't see the show with you lot in your street clothes. Lets get you into your rehearsal dresses. *(He runs to the back of the room to pick them up)*
Now I've seen the real things and man are they fantastic. So lets change into them please

He starts to hand them out

RUFUS   Ladies if you could kindly change into them immediately

PEPSI   What here?

RUFUS   As much as that would be nice, (looking to MAY) there are changing room round there to the left.

PEPSI   Respect.

RUFUS   Hurry up. Come back and parade for me, yeah?

RUFUS   (He turns to the band) Now you guys are gonna be all in electric blue!

Rufus' mobile rings

RUFUS   Yo Adelle ! Whats happenin baby?

Julie shakes her head and expresses her feelings about Rufus through the beautiful Maxine Brown song.

OH NO NOT MY BABY

It is sung with much irony
The song ends and Julie exits the stage.

Orletta returns to the stage with her long sequenced black dress.

RUFUS   Alright I'll call you tomorrow, bye. Orletta, you look wonderful, I nearly mistook you for a woman you know

ORLETTA   Very funny, ha ha.

RUFUS   No seriously, how do you feel?

ORLETTA   I have worn a dress before you know

RUFUS   Good then you'll know how to move in it.

ORLETTA   They're a bit restrictive. What about all those men's moves ?

RUFUS   Yer, good point, I've been thinking about that. Maybe you could put on a bowler hats or something and then pull up the skirts...

Rufus touches the dress

ORLETTA   Take yer hands off my body!

RUFUS   Erh. Can you go and try on the other shoes I bought.

ORLETTA   Yer

She leaves. Enter Pepsi. She looks great but because it is figure hugging feels a little embarrassed about revealing her physique.

RUFUS   Yes Pepsi, ah you that rude girl? How do you feel?

PEPSI   A bit exposed

RUFUS   Rubbish, I can't see a bit of your body, bar of course that tantalising flash of leg

She quickly looks down. She tries to regain street cool

RUFUS   Do think you can move in it?

PEPSI   Yes, I just have get use to it innit...............

RUFUS   Hell Yeah!

Enter Maylica who has taken the longest to get into her outfit. She looks stunning. We can see that Rufus is affected

RUFUS	Eh, Pepsi can you go and practice that walk in the corridor.
PEPSI	OK
RUFUS	You look ...... stunning.
MAY	Thank you
	Rufus wonders over to where Maylika's sitting. He wants to talk to her bad. The first thing out of his mouth is:
RUFUS	You feel comfortable in that?
MAYLIKA	Yes I do, look forward to the real thing
RUFUS	Yeah so do I. Maylika, why have you been distant with me today ?
MAYLIKA	Have I ?
RUFUS	You can't answer a question with a question
MAYLIKA	I just did
RUFUS	Well your not supposed to.
MAYLIKA	Who said ?
RUFUS	This is getting me nowhere is it ?
MAYLIKA	No it's not
RUFUS	Alright one nil to you.
MAYLIKA	Let me ask you a personal question?
RUFUS	No I'm really sorry. I can't have your babies.
MAYLIKA	Is that what you want, to be a cruise boat cabaret artist?
RUFUS	Well maybe not for the rest of my life but about the next fifty years or so would be cool.
MAYLIKA	Why? You can achieve much more.
RUFUS	(*Being sarcastic*) What like be number one in the hit parade?

MAYLIKA   Why not?

RUFUS   Oh girl, I'm too old for that marlakey

Rufus pauses for a while deciding whether to go deeper. After a beat or so he decides to go with it

RUFUS   Of Course I use to wanna be a pop star. Who didn't? I tried, but it never seemed to work. So the idea of a steady income in the sun as oppose to hustling gig to gig, girl that sounds so good to me.

MAYLIKA   I think you should never give up your dreams.

RUFUS   I think you watch too many American chat shows.

Orletta enters and sees Rufus trying to sweet talk Maylika.

RUFUS   All right every body. Where's Pepsi please. Can we kick into SOS, moves and everything. Orletta are you up to speed on this number?

ORLETTA   Nearly

RUFUS   Well just do as much as you can

ORLETTA   Thank you

RUFUS   Steve count us off when your ready. Girls remember Be butch, you're men!.

The girls look at each other and raise their eyes to the heavens.

STEVE   1 2 3 4

The band kick into the Edwin Starr number from the top. They are now the Temptations. The girls are the other three members and Rufus is the lead singer. The choreography is pure old tempts.

STOP HER ON SIGHT

The song ends

During the song Pepsi gets some of the moves wrong

RUFUS   Pepsi I think you need to concentrate on the moves a little more don't you? Take five while I go over some arrangements with Steve.

Rufus walks to Steve at the piano. The girls relax to their chairs. Maylika once again gets out her mobile to check her messages

MAYLIKA   Well done Orletta.

PEPSI   Yes, you only started this morning and you were better than me. I messed up loads of times.

ORLETTA   You were fine. Have confidence girl

MAYLIKA   Damn, no messages

ORLETTA   Girl, I see a few sparks flying between you and Rufus…

MAY   I don't think so, he's not my type

PEPSI   Really?! I think he's well fit. Don't you Orletta?

ORLETTA   I wouldn't be seen dead with that man if the choice was between him and Bernard Manning

MAY   Bernard Manning has got a little something you know!

PEPSI   Yeah? What?

MAY   Money. Those old time comedians have loot! And child I don't work so hard to be fine, to rest my behind, on the back seat of a Austin Rover, know what I'm saying!

SISTERS   (*Laugh*). You are so bad!

PEPSI   But it's true. Woman cannot live by bread alone!!!!!

She decides to burst her bubble

MAY   What you know about bread alone church girl. You even had a man?

PEPSI   Of course I have. And don't be calling me no church girl I'm a rude gal.

Orletta pause to look at Pepsi quizzingly

ORLETTA   You lie! You ain't never had a man?

She struggles to answer

PEPSI   I... I.....

MAY   A twenty year old virgin. You'd be worth a lot of money in some parts of Africa

PEPSI   (*Emphatically*) I've had boyfriends and dat!

MAY   Yeah but you ain't never done 'the Nasty'!

Pepsi kisses her teeth

Maylica starts to laugh. Both women converge on Pepsi and start to demonstrate the next passage

MAY   Phew girl you don't know what you missing. (*She begins to recall*) That gentle....

ORLETTA   Soggy.........

MAY   Kiss on the neck. The caressing of the breast

Orletta mimes twisting her breast as if tuning her radio

ORLETTA   As if he's tuning into Radio one.

MAY   That hand slowly sliding, reaching, touching that .....

ORLETTA   Steady.........

MAY   And finally he's there.......and before you know it........

ORLETTA   It's over. Um hm. Keep that shit to yourself I say. That's what I'd do if I had it all to live again

MAY   Orletta, you have just not tasted the real sweetness of man

ORLETTA   Damn right. There are too many crusty ones out there, mate

PEPSI   The only man that don't break hearts is Jesus Christ

The girls look at each other and smile. Maylika moves on

ORLETTA There ain't much you can say to that

MAY What I'm really looking for is a stinking rich man to sweep me off my feet and say "MAYLICA, I know you're an independent woman of the 2K's but let- me - look after you". Oh yeah.

ORLETTA But that's just like, the lottery with a shag!

MAY And if you don't play you can't win!

ORLETTA So you're gonna just sit there and wait for some man to look after you for the rest of your days?

MAYLIKA Don't take yourself so seriously Girl, I never take my eyes off the prize.

She thinks for a second before continuing

MAYLIKA I got someone coming in tonight actually

PEPSI Really? Who?

MAYLIKA An old buddy who has just become head of AnR at EMI.

PEPSI What is he gonna give you a recording contract?

ORLETTA Off what you're doing in this show?

Maylika ignores her and continues talking to Pepsi.

MAYLIKA He promised me that I'd be his first signing, and so he's bringing his boss to see me tonight to ok the deal.

ORLETTA How long have you been in this business? I can't believe you fell for that one. His first signing. (*She chuckles*). Did he say that before or after the blow job…

MAYLIKA Orletta I don't know what your problem is but please don't put your negativity on me.

ORLETTA I ain't putting nothing on you, but if you gonna believe a man when he tells you that jazz then you gotta lot a learning to do

MAYLIKA	Maybe you should focus on your own career a little more instead of taking your bitterness out on us who are trying to keep our hopes alive.

Orletta looks at her and then kisses her teeth.

Enter Rufus.

RUFUS	What's all this kissing and nashing of teeth?

No body replies

RUFUS	I didn't see any you going through your moves or your harmonies. Call me old fashioned but time is money and the money is mine? Seeing that you're all so on it, Pepsi show me the moves.

Pepsi looks to the other girls frightened

RUFUS	What you looking at them for, they don't know your moves! Come on 1234

Pepsi starts the moves and then gets it wrong

PEPSI	Sorry Mr Rufus
RUFUS	(*Shouting*) I don't understand what is wrong with you. They're three simple steps.
ORLETTA	You don't have to shout at her
RUFUS	I am not shouting. We have a show tonight. Not tomorrow, but tonight. After three days rehearsal I expect this shit to be one whole lot better than that. What am I paying my money for? Get it together

He steams off

ORLETTA	Ignore him Pepsi. Idiot. You were doing fine.
PEPSI	It's ok I understand. When he gets angry he shouts
MAYLIKA	Excuse me a second

Maylika leaves to speak to Rufus upstage. Pepsi turns to Orletta

PEPSI   I'm really don't feel comfortable dancing. (*She catches herself*) I mean I'm cool when I'm in the dance hall and dat, but when it comes to this stage bizness stuff I freeze up.

ORLETTA   Child of course you can dance, look. Big tart, little tart Diva! Watch!

Orletta breaks into a dance routine. Suddenly the lights change and we are in the world of Orletta and Pepsi. Orletta starts to sing the funky Aretha version bang on the verse. The band kicks off with her.

ROCK STEADY

As the song progresses Pepsi becomes more confident. She is now enjoying it. She throws her hands up in the air and waves them like she just don't care

ORLETTA   Now try to Wilson Pickett

Pepsi does the dance break and is really good

The number finishes. The lights change back to normal and Pepsi hugs Orletta.

ORLETTA   See, what did I tell you?

PEPSI   Thank you, that was wicked. (*She pauses for thought and then asks*) Orletta, what's it like being a star?

ORLETTA   Oh baby I ain't no star.

PEPSI   'Course you are. You've been on T.O.P and all that stuff. (*Confiding in her*) You know, I plan to be a star one day

Orletta shakes her head and smiles

ORLETTA   Why'd a nice girl like you wanna go and do a thing like that?

PEPSI   Because it's all I've ever wanted. And I've got a wicked angle, Orletta. I'm gonna merge my natural London street persona, with, wait for it gospel music. Not that I'm religious or anything. Cool huh?

ORLETTA   Em, very

Pepsi is a little embarrassed but slowly goes for it

PEPSI Yeah! I plan to be the first artist to bring Raga Gospel to the masses. (*Growing in confidence*) I'm going to be Shaggy meets Aretha

Orletta stifles a laugh

PEPSI What are you laughing at?

ORLETTA (*Quoting the song*) It wasn't me

Pepsi quickly continues she's on a flow now

PEPSI I'm gonna be Madonna meets Mahalia Jackson, James Brown meets Ziggy Marley, yes I'm going to be a Pop gospel.. (*She struggles to find the word*) superstar.

Orletta does laugh this time

PEPSI What you laughing at?

ORLETTA I'm not laughing honestly, but you know be careful who you say that to, some people might think you're taking drugs.

PEPSI (*Outraged*) Drugs! (*Concerned*) I know that I have to establish myself first, but that's why this gig is so important to me. It's my first rung up the ladder of success.

ORLETTA (*Hunting her out*) Is every track gonna be a gospel?

PEPSI Yep

ORLETTA Oh child. You know how many church divas I've heard say (*Imitating*) "I'm gonna give glory to God on every track of my album" and before you've made two hit records they're shagging the producer and snorting cocaine in the back of his Lexus

She shakes his head

PEPSI I can tell you for sure I ain't gonna be like that

ORLETTA You know what, I believe you. I really do. But girl when you've been in the business as long as I have….I tell you…

PEPSI Well it's a new century. Things are going to be different.

ORLETTA   I hope so lass, but there's a long road ahead you

She turns and walks away

PEPSI   God. What am I doing !?

Enter a very worried looking Julie who runs straight up to Orletta.

ORLETTA   What's up girl? You look pale!

JULIE   Have you had a chance to run over your numbers with Steve and the band?

ORLETTA   Well he's looked at it, but we haven't gone through it properly cos er Rufus came in.

Julie is a little flustered she speaks over Orletta

JULIE   Ok I'll have to engineer a way to get him out and then you and the band quickly run through them.

ORLETTA   All right but what's wrong?

JULIE   I'll tell you later.

Julie walks up to Maylika and Rufus

JULIE   Sorry to disturb this lovely little gathering but can I have a word with you please.

He attempts to open his mouth but before his lips can part;

JULIE   Now.

RUFUS   Excuse me Maylika. Yes my love.

JULIE   The P n O people just called. They can't make it tomorrow night.

RUFUS   What?

JULIE   Something's cropped up and the only time they can do it is tonight

RUFUS   They can't see it tonight. It's under rehearsed.

JULIE   I know, I know, I tried....

RUFUS   ...Call them back. Tell them they *have* to come tomorrow night.

JULIE   I tried to tell them that....

RUFUS   Well try harder. Tell them one of the singers has lost they're voice. Tell them one of the band has lost a hand.

JULIE   RUFUS. You are not listening to me. It's tonight or not at all.

RUFUS   Oh for fish cake sake.

JULIE   And there's one other thing.

RUFUS   What? They want me to do bloody Elvis impressions?

JULIE   They've kinda changed the mind on what they're looking for. What they really want is an act that spans all the generations, not just one

RUFUS   But they know I'm a sixties act

JULIE   I know, but they were just giving me a word of advice. They said if we could somehow fit some up to date songs into the act, as well as some dance numbers we'd stand a really good chance of getting the gig.

RUFUS   They're out of order.

JULIE   They're not asking you to do transcendental hip house ambient trance tracks, just something from the seventies or eighties.

RUFUS   They either take me as I am or not at all. Finite

Julie tries to placate him

JULIE   We need this gig Ruf. YOU need this gig. You need to think about this.

RUFUS   Think about what? What am I gonna do? Pull a new repertoire out of my arse...

JULIE   (*As if new idea*) Get the girls to do the eighties numbers. That way you wouldn't have to do it and it would still be in the act. I'm sure that Orletta must know.....

RUFUS Are you crazy? That way if I get the gig I got to take her with me! Hell no! You tell them that they gonna see what we told them they'd see. Rufus Collins and his sixties soul act. Now I'm going off to try and get this boat ship shape.

JULIE Don't you walk away from me. You don't get this gig and it's over.

RUFUS What do you mean over?

JULIE I mean that I've given 110% and I don't know how much more I've got left to give, this gig is important to me.

RUFUS So what? You're gonna give me my papers?

JULIE I'm simply saying that if you get this gig you won't be needing me as much. I gotta start thinking about me, my future.

RUFUS Julie, you do what you got to do, you hear, and so will I. PHONE THEM !

He walks off back into the rehearsal space. He is in a bad mood but will not tell them why.

RUFUS Right everybody. Steve what's the next number in the set?

STEVE The letter

RUFUS Lets do it please.

STEVE Cool. Bands ready!

RUFUS Girls? Can we take two seconds to think about the moves in this number. I can't tell you how much I need this to be tight.

ORLETTA Are we boys or girls?

RUFUS You're girls. Try your best

The song kicks into gear. It is their own version of Joe Cocker great song THE LETTER. The girls doing a slick girly routine. Rufus sings lead

THE LETTER

The song ends. It's kicked ass

RUFUS   (*Being anal*) Steve could you guys look over the middle section, it wasn't quite firing. Ronnie less of the flashing lights mate. Its not a discotheque!

STEVE   Yeah yeah. Guys lets go to bar fifteen.

The girls are nackered. Julie has been looking at the number. She claps at the end

RUFUS   That was good girls

GIRLS   Thank you

RUFUS   Yeah right, don't get conceited, while they're doing that, start thinking about the next number please

Julie walks past Orletta

JULIE   Orletta, If he doesn't budge I'm in trouble girl

ORLETTA   Let me try an angle

JULIE   Be careful

Rufus spots Julie

RUFUS   Yeah yeah, one minute. Orletta

RUFUS   Have you called them yet?

JULIE   Yeah

RUFUS   What did they say?

JULIE   Answer phone

RUFUS   Damn

JULIE   Look I've got to run to the bank. Oh Ann Marie just called and said that the costumes have to be picked up in the next thirty. I can't do both. So you're gonna have to do it?

RUFUS   Can't she put them in a cab or something?

JULIE   Are you gonna trust all of that to a minicab driver that you don't know? Anything could happen

RUFUS   Ah man. All right I'll do it, but I swear they're a conspiracy going on to stop me getting this gig. It's just one thing after the other. What number does Ann Marie live at again?

Julie gives him the address on a piece of paper

JULIE   See you later

Rufus goes back to get his jacket and stuff.

ORLETTA   Rufus , can I speak to you a minute please? I don't mean to be funny but this band is firing. You know there's a huge audience out there for more up to date material, like you know, the seventies

RUFUS   You're taking the piss right?

ORLETTA   No. What you need is a little Chaka Khan and James Brown in the act. Then come right up to date and do a Destiny's Child number.

RUFUS   A who number?

ORLETTA   Destiny's Child you know (*singing the hook*) I'm a survivor, I'm gonna make it I will survive, keep on surviving.

He obviously doesn't know it

ORLETTA   Be more militant, adventurous. We could even do a little Bob Marley!

RUFUS   Bob who!....Have you quite finished?

ORLETTA   Yes

Rufus gets passionate

RUFUS   Let me tell you something young lady, there is <u>nothing</u> more adventurous than the sounds of the '60's. It was those bands that took the bull by it's horns so that you, and your "'surviving!...." acts could even be thought about, so don't you talk to me about militant. These songs are the embodiment of militant

ORLETTA   I know that Rufus but that was then, and this is........

RUFUS   That's where your wrong see, this <u>is</u> the music of today, yesterday, and tomorrow. These are real songs, not no electronic bleeping with screaming on top, not no thumping bass drum with men shouting obscenities, but music where you can smell the soul. Soul is to hear Jesus Orletta. Don't tell me about today's music, cos all I hear is the devil.

ORLETTA So, you disagree then?

RUFUS Yes I do. And I am fed up of everybody trying to tell me what I should be doing with my act. This band is called Rufus Collins and his '60's Soul band. That's what I'm paying for and that's the way it's gonna stay. Any one got a problem with that knows what they can do

ORLETTA What crap. Since when have you been loyal to anything but yourself?

RUFUS I'm sorry

ORLETTA You, the original self serving sell out, loyal to the sixties?!

RUFUS Listen.......

ORLETTA No you listen. You don't love the sixties Rufus, you're a fraud. You're afraid to compete with the new boys. They're younger, finer and stronger than you are and you can't take it. Well you can hide from the others but I know you as the sucker that left Julie and I flat on our faces so that you could run off and be a superstar. But where are you now Mr Cabaret 2001? I tell you where you are, you're back to being the coward that has always missed the big picture. Carry on, you're gonna be doing this same shit in 10 years time.

Rufus just stares at her. When she has finished. He looks around the rehearsal room. Every one is staring at them.

(To all)
RUFUS Ladies and gentlemen, I'm going to pick up our costumes. Steve, take the band and the girls through the rest of the set for me. Orletta if you're still here when I come back. I'll take that to mean your going to do the show the way I want it. If you're not here. Believe me I'll understand. Anybody got a problem with that?

ALL No

He exits. Orletta crosses over to Steve. Maylika gets out her mobile to check for messages

ORLETTA   You know what, I'm gonna take my arse home

When it is clear that Rufus has left the building Julie creeps back on the stage.

JULIE   Orletta, Orletta. You're doing this for me remember.

ORLETTA   Yeah, I remember, but..

JULIE   Please.

Orletta kisses her teeth

JULIE   Okay, lets rehearse these new numbers before he gets back.

MAYLIKA   What are you doing?

JULIE   Just saving someone's life and putting an end to my own.

MAYLIKA   Shouldn't we be rehearsing the numbers from the show?

JULIE   Don't worry I'm sure your number will be fine.

*The band kick into eight bars of Grace Jones '**Pull up to the bumper**' Orletta sings the first verse*

ORLETTA   Alright. See what I'm saying this band is kicking. When you get the gist of that one, lets try this emotions number, then I got a couple a Chaka Khans, a little Lauren Hill

JULIE   Woo

As that song has finished Orletta shouts

ORLETTA   Yeah, line up the next ones boys

As she finishes the last word of that sentence Rufus walks back in. he's forgotten his keys. Some coughs out

Everyone stands shocked for a moment. Did he hear them rehearsing. He takes off his head set.
He looks around at all the guilty looking faces.

RUFUS   That's what I like to hear?

JULIE   What's what you like to hear?

RUFUS   When I took off my head set Orletta was asking for the next number to be lined up. Glad to see that professionalism has finally descended. Carry on with the good work people.

Rufus picks up his keys explaining what he is doing back. He exits again. The girls fall about laughing

JULIE   Oh we will……

BLACK OUT .END OF ACT ONE

TABS FALL. JULIE IS IN SPOTLIGHT.

JULIE   Ladies and gentlemen, in my capacity as manager I've have negotiated that while we rehearse the stage to be yours for the next fifteen minutes. So I want you to get up here on the stage and boogie with us until Rufus gets back.

THE BAND KICK INTO THE INTERVAL SET.

Act Two.

SCENE ONE

Lights come half way up. The curtain is in. We can hear the conversation between the characters going on via mic's. We see Julie run back stage from front of house she has a bunch of flowers in her hand

JULIE Okay let's get started the PnO people have arrived.

RUFUS Are they in a good mood?

JULIE They look like they're here to party

RUFUS Oh who sent me the flowers?

JULIE Eh, they're not for you, they were sent for me.

RUFUS Oh yeah, who sent you those then?

JULIE A friend!

RUFUS A friend? You sleeping with him

JULIE Rufus.

RUFUS Yeah yeah okay guys, lets focus and remember why were here, were here to make me look good. Only kidding. Lets focus lets go out there guy and lets party! Start that drum roll

The drum roll begins the lights change and Rufus puts on his corny American accent

RUFUS Ladies and gentlemen, are you ready? I said are you ready? Husbands hold your wives, wives leaves your husbands, the moment you've been waiting for has arrived. Ladies and gentlemen give it up for Rufus Collins and his all star soul band

The band kicks into Sam and Dave's 'Soul man'. The curtain rises. He, the gals and the band are kicked out in fantastic costumes. They kick into a mad and bad routine.

SOUL MAN

*We segway into **SOUL SISTER BROWN SUGAR** by Sam and Dave*

The song ends and moves straight into Otis Reddings;

TRY A LITTLE TENDERNESS

The song ends

RUFUS While I go off and slip into something a little cooler, My girls led by Sister Maylika gonna show you a little respect

Maylica runs to the front of the stage, grabs the mic and hits into Aretha's;

RESPECT

During the last part of Respect it becomes obvious that something wrong with Orletta. She is clearly looking out into the audience. Suddenly she breaks into a big smile as if she's seen what she's been looking for. Orletta stops singing and dancing which in turn stops the other girls.

ORLETTA Stop. STOPPPPPP.

The band slowly wind down to a halt. She goes into a fake routine

ORLETTA I can't take this no more.

They all stare at her in disbelief, horror and amazement.

ORLETTA Oh it's all quiet. Look I love this stuff an all but I sing these songs year in year out. I'm sorry girls but I need to get funky man.

She turns to the audience

ORLETTA Can we take you somewhere else?

MAY What do you think you are doing?

She ignores her

ORLETTA	Anybody out there mind if we get a little funky down here?

We get a slight murmur from the audience

ORLETTA	I don't care Stixs, I'm gonna count you off. Hit me with one of those funky songs

*Steve, looks at Dave, who shrugs his shoulders, and then kicks into a funky beat. it is the intro to **'Do you love what you feel'** by Chaka khan.*

ORLETTA	Yeah I feel that. Dave (*bass*) Gimme a little something!

Dave the bass player comes in with the bad bass line

To audience

ORLETTA	You might as well clap your hands, I know you can feel it. Come on clap with me.

She starts the audience off clapping

ORLETTA	Come on Soul Sisters, are you with me?

Pepsi and Maylica look at each other. Maylika is fuming. It was her number that she ruined the end of.

SISTERS	Yeah, we with you (*With different attitudes*)

ORLETTA	Then lets make this funky

The three sisters rip off part of their dress to reveal a funky, if a little makeshift, outfit
The full band kicks into the number. It's the cooking Chaka Khan and Rufus Song

DO YOU LOVE WHAT YOU FEEL

At the end of the verse Rufus runs onto stage three quarters dressed. He is in general shock at the goings on, but he realises that he would look like a fool if he suddenly stopped it.

Realising that he is on stage Orletta throws Rufus the mic.

ORLETTA   Rufus Collins, ladies and gentlemen, the **Original** Soul Man! Sing the thang, Rufus!!

He is forced to sing the second verse.

The number goes on for another verse and Chorus and when Rufus thinks the time is right he wraps the band off. The number ends. Orletta is feeling in control now.

ORLETTA   Did you like that?

The audience shout back 'yer'

ORLETTA   Did you love what you felt. Gimme a oh yeah!

The audience shout back 'oh yer'

As the song is finishing he speaks over the music

RUFUS   We're just gonna take a short break to sort out a slight technical hitch and then we'll be back with some more searing sounds of the sixties. So don't go away.

The curtain drops.

SCENE TWO

When it rises we are in the side stage area. Orletta the girls and the band are standing heads down awaiting the big explosion. Rufus is silent for a few seconds and then he explodes

RUFUS   What the freak do you think you lot are doing!

ORLETTA   Look Rufus I'm sorry I was just trying to give the show some life.

RUFUS   Life?!!! You wanted to give my show life?

He loses it

RUFUS   You must want me to beat…!!!

She cuts in on him, Orletta is certainly not afraid of him

ORLETTA   What? Come on then, I'm not of afraid you, you wimp.

RUFUS	Know how much was at stake for me tonight you punk?
ORLETTA	I don't care. Now you know how I felt when you walked out on Julie and I. Believe ,you pick the wrong woman to mess with.
RUFUS	Woman? You're not a woman, you're a man, you masculine wanna be
ORLETTA	Masculine wanna be? Huh look whose talking, you ain't nothing but a pussy in pants
RUFUS	What? Pussy in pa… Look at you, I bet you ain't ever had a man?
ORLETTA	How dare you question my parts, bastard

Julie runs onto stage screaming

JULIE	Orletta! What the hell did you do that for?
ORLETTA	Julie tell this man that you…

Orletta is stunned

ORLETTA	What?
JULIE	Why did you stop the show?
ORLETTA	Because you told me too
JULIE	I did not. I told you I would give you the sign
ORLETTA	I saw you waving your hands in the air so I went for it.
JULIE	Waving my hands? I was dancing you fool
RUFUS	You told Orletta to take over my show?
JULIE	I didn't tell her to do that Rufus
ORLETTA	Of course you did. Think I bought my sheet music because its good lunch time reading?
JULIE	I said I was going to tell Rufus in the interval that we'd rehearsed the songs and then if he still refused that then we might….

ORLETTA   You did not….

JULIE   …That's what I said

ORLETTA   Don't you be lying on me now to my face!

Pepsi screams at the top of her voice

PEPSI   Hold it .

JULIE   Be quiet and sit down. Oh my word, I just ran straight back here I forgot all about the P n O people. I'll be back

As angry as she is at Orletta cutting her number Maylika realises that her wages are at risk so decides to try and make it not as bad as it is

MAY   Rufus it was out of order but, the people seem to like it

RUFUS   Like it? That unrehearsed, sham of an act? You were like three stage school girls on heat. Yeah well I hope you had fun because you three ain't gonna get nich else from this gig, I tell ya

All three girls turn their heads towards Rufus sharply and sharply shout

GIRLS   What?

ORLETTA   What do you mean by that?

RUFUS   Exactly what I said. It's your gig now Orletta go on pay the people na!

ORLETTA   What! I ain't got no money

RUFUS   Oh you wanna go breaking contract and not take the responsibilities

ORLETTA   Contract? I never signed no contract

RUFUS   Oh yes you did, a verbal one. And that contract said that you were to perform as the Soul Sisters in Rufus Collins '60's tribute band. Tonight you performed as yourselves. That spells NO MONEY in my book

MAY   I knew that pompous git would do this

RUFUS   What did you call me?

MAY   Rufus Come On ! . Lets just go back out there and do it as we rehearsed.

RUFUS   Do what? My stale old sixties songs! Sorry, your apologies to late mate, should have thought of that before you started ripping off your clothes.

          Enter Stuart who whispers in Rufus's ear

RUFUS   The management want to see me.

          They exit

MAY   Well thank you Orletta, this gig was my gas bill.

ORLETTA   I'm sorry............ (*still humble*) but I thought that I was doing what Julie asked me to do.

MAYLIKA   In the middle of my number? I'm gonna go and see if my recording people are still out there. If you've messed that up for me Orletta, it's not Rufus you've got to be worried about I can tell you.

          She exits

ORLETTA   Ooo. She's a bit touchy!

PEPSI   Of course she is. You've ruined our careers! I'm finished on my first gig.

ORLETTA   Don't be silly, no ones heard of Rufus Collins. That's why he's does gigs like this!

PEPSI   My boss at work had.

ORLETTA   You're career will be fine Pepsi.

PEPSI   My names not Pepsi its Mary Cumberbatch and I'm a pastors daughter from Harrow. I had one chance to get onto the ladder of success and now you've just kicked it away.

ORLETTA   For a pastors daughter you sure can lie!

Pepsi sits at the Piano. We go into her world she begins to sing and play a personalised version of Jimmy Cliffs

MANY RIVERS TO CROSS

Orletta enters her own world and together they spilt the second verse and Chorus

The song ends

Pepsi gets up and excuses herself

PEPSI   Excuse me for a minute, I'm just gonna go to the ladies.

She exits in a hurry.

Enter Maylika. She is really down. Her recording exec obviously wasn't there they clock each other.

ORLETTA   Hey Maylika, was he there?

MAYLIKA   No!

ORLETTA   Listen I'm so sorry…

MAYLIKA   You should be. Maybe it's for my good. (*Pulling herself together*) Maybe a bigger Something's around the corner

ORLETTA   I wish I could be that optimistic

MAYLIKA   About what?

ORLETTA   About everything.

Maylika is surprised to hear this side of Orletta

MAYLIKA   But you've had a great life. You've travelled the world, you've seen your music at number one, you've learnt a living. Girl you've had everything I've ever wanted

ORLETTA   Living? I only took this gig to poke fun at Rufus. I mean when it comes to that you know you've hit rock bottom. I'm brok na backside

MAYLIKA   Didn't I read somewhere once that you got a kid? She must bring you joy?

She's hit a sore point. Orletta pauses before answering

ORLETTA   No, I don't. it was a publicity stunt. If I wasn't single I swear I'd be working in Tesco's.

MAYLIKA   It's never to late.

ORLETTA   What to work in Tescos?

MAYLIKA   No, to have babies

ORLETTA   Sugar it ain't the organs I'm worrying about, it's the man. You got any good ones spare?

She's hit a sore point. Maylika pauses before answering

MAYLIKA   I don't have one for myself. Still I got a good couple of months out of the last one

ORLETTA   Damn I got food in my fridge that's older than that. Girl we one sad pair of boots

The smile a smile of recognition with each other

MAYLIKA   Have hope Orletta. You did it once you can do it again

ORLETTA   Yeah. But I got twenty years on the girl who took the charts by storm.

MAYLIKA   If you don't believe, how you gonna expect anyone else too?

ORLETTA   That's just the thing, I don't know if I want any one else too. The thrill has gone. Work, men. I give up.

Rufus walks back in. Maylika spot's him.

RUFUS   Well thank you every body. The management have just cancelled the rest of the gig, and their not going to pay.

MAYLIKA   They've done what?

RUFUS   Not that I can blame them, I'd have done the same

JOHHNY   No more music?

RUFUS   No more music.

JOHHNY   Better pack up boys

ORLETTA   Rufus I am so sorry. I feel terrible. Look do you want back the money you paid me in advance?

RUFUS   Yep

ORLETTA   Can I get it to you some time next week? I spent most of it.

RUFUS   What a fantastic gesture Orletta, I should be suing your arse

ORLETTA   I've said I'm sorry Rufus I can't do any more

RUFUS   None of you lot knew how much tonight meant to me. I hope I don't ever see any of your ugly faces again

Enter a very excited Julie. She sees the musicians packing up

JULIE   What you doing? Don't pack up are you mad?

STEVE   Rufus said.....

JULIE   Rufus they loved it. The P n O people loved it. They thought it was all part of the show. They can't wait to see the second half.

RUFUS   Second half? You expect us to work wonders and shit miracles in five minutes?

They all look at Orletta. She looks away with guilt

RUFUS   Oh don't tell me

They all look to Orletta. She reluctantly replies

ORLETTA   Well we had rehearsed a couple?

RUFUS   Rehearsed! I don't believe you people!

PEPSI   Lets kick off that Emotions number we rehearsed, let the boss do the Stevie Wonder or Teddy Pendergrass and wrap up with one of your Chaka Khans Orletta.

They stare at Pepsi in amazement.

ALL   Ah you dat Pepsi.

PEPSI   No this is Mary in full effect. Now if we take some of the dance steps from the numbers we no longer need, adapt them to the new ones….

RUFUS   Oh yeah and how do we do that?

PEPSI   With the emotions number, do Sam Cooke dance break. The Teddy Pendergrass, with Four tops moves, and we all just vibe the Chaka Khan. . My mothers a pastor you know, organising is in my genes.

GIRLS   Yeah

RUFUS   Hellooooooooo

ORLETTA   Oh sorry, are you happy with Pepsi's suggestions Rufus?

Trying to get back in control

RUFUS   Steve, you and the boys have heard the new set I've arranged. You cool with that?

STEVE   Cool

The band exit

RUFUS   I can't take this, I feel like I'm in one of those 40's musicals.

JULIE   Yeah well you better get a grip and do it

RUFUS   Alright guys, lets go out there and get

(*He struggles to say it*)

JULIE   Mordeney!

RUFUS   Moderny! Lets do it

SCENE THREE

When they snap back up we are 'on stage'. we are gonna gig for a bit. the girls are standing in a pose. The band breaks for a few beats.

RUFUS   People are you ready? People are you ready to jam?

They reply

*The band break into the emotions **BEST OF MY LOVE**.*

As the song ends we segway into the Harold Melvin and the Blue Note classic
DON'T LEAVE ME THIS WAY

Rufus sings the lead

The song ends and we kick straight into the Chaka Khan Classic

AIN'T NOBODY

Rufus joins the other sisters in back up. They start a smooth dance routine. Pepsi really sells the first verse. The other girls sing the second and third

As the song ends Rufus and the sisters dance off the stage.

The band finish the number and we go to

Blackout

SCENE FOUR

The stage after the gig is over and the audience has gone home. Rufus is sat on the stage alone. He has changed his clothes for home. Maylika walks onto the stage and sees him.

MAYLIKA   What you doing here Rufus. You should be out there greeting your fans. The show was great.

RUFUS   It was the biggest fiasco I have ever been involved in

MAYLIKA   Yeah, but the audience loved it. And that's all that counts.

RUFUS   Not to me. Anyway, what about your guy that was coming? Did he enjoy it?

MAYLIKA   I don't think he came.

RUFUS   Are you and he kinda romantically linked.

MAYLIKA   Oh no.

Beat

MAYLIKA   Why?

RUFUS   Oh nothing. Where's the other girls?

MAYLIKA   Well Pepsi's out front, And I left Orletta in the changing room.

RUFUS   Right.

They pause. she makes to leave. They both want to say something to each other but cannot find the way in. Finally they both bite the bullet at the same time

RUFUS   Maylika

MAY   Rufus ………

BOTH   Sorry

BOTH   No you go ahead

They both laugh

RUFUS   I remember what I was going say, after you

MAY   No really, I insist

Beat

RUFUS   I want to apologise, when I said I didn't want to see any of you again, it wasn't the truth.

She is silent

RUFUS   But if you don't want to see me again, I dig it. That me and Orletta thing ! It was out of order. I'm sorry

Maylica is still silent

RUFUS   What were you going to say?

MAY   Nothing, except that I'm sorry for calling you a pompous git. I didn't mean it. You're a prat but I'm quite fond of you really

RUFUS Really?

MAY Really.

They get closer

RUFUS Thank you for that. It means a lot to me.

They are in kissing range. They move in and....

Enter Julie. she sees this and makes her presence felt. She sings

JULIE You can't hurry love, no you just have to wait, love don't come easy, it's a game of give and take.

Big embarrassment all around. Maylika ups and leaves

JULIE Nothing changes I see. Still knocking off the employees? Now you see that's why I's gotta go!

He can say nothing

JULIE Well do you want to know the score?

RUFUS That would be good?

JULIE They liked it, they liked it a lot.

Rufus jumps up and punches the air

RUFUS I told you, I told you.

JULIE Calm down a second. You haven't heard the rest

RUFUS The rest? What rest?

Julie doesn't know how to say this

JULIE They liked the show, but they didn't like you

RUFUS What do you mean they didn't like me? How can you like the show and not like me? I am the freaking show.

JULIE I know but you weren't tonight. Tonight the girls were the centre of the show.

RUFUS   So what exactly are you saying here?

JULIE   I'm saying that they liked the girls

RUFUS   They liked the girls?

JULIE   Yes, they liked the girls

RUFUS   So where does that leave me?

JULIE   Black and broke. Only kidding. It means that the act they want to book is one that features Orletta, Maylika and Pepsi.

RUFUS   But they didn't come here to see the girls

           He is getting mad and kicking things

JULIE   We've been here already Rufus

RUFUS   I don't care. I got to get this straight in my head. I work my bollocks off performing in this shit, and they want the girls and not me to go off on their frigging cruise ship?

JULIE   That's about the sum of it. Yes.

RUFUS   Well isn't that freaking great to fish cake corner.

JULIE   There's no need to swear

RUFUS   And I bet that you've gone and brokered that deal haven't you?

JULIE   Um, (*She gulps*) That's what I've come back stage to talk to YOU ALL about.

           Enter Pepsi and Orletta as if by magic, they've been listening at the door

ORLETTA   Talk to us? What about?

JULIE   Well, (*She looks to Rufus, he nods as if to say carry on*) we had some scouts from a huge cruise company in tonight, and they were very keen to see if, you, the girls, and the band would be interested in maybe doing your act on one of their cruisers.

ORLETTA   But we haven't got an act?

PEPSI   And what about Rufus? Don't they want him too?

JULIE   I'll come back to that. They thought what you did tonight was your act. And I told them that it was.

ORLETTA   Damn. Is the money good?

JULIE   Yeah

PEPSI   And where does it, this cruiser I mean, where does it go?

JULIE   All over the world.

RUFUS   I've had enough.

JULIE   Rufus sit down, I'll get to you in minute. Pepsi will you do me a favour and go find Maylika, she's probably wrapped around the most expensive man in the room, we need to talk this out now. They want to come and see the show again tomorrow night

RUFUS   What! I'm not doing this crap again?

JULIE   We are still under contract. Orletta, how do you feel in principal about this

RUFUS   Principal? Huh!

JULIE   Rufus

ORLETTA   I don't know Julie. I haven't really thought about it. And I feel kinda bad about Rufus.

They all stare at her

ORLETTA   A bit

JULIE   Well, here's what I propose for tomorrow night

Lights down

SCENE FIVE

During the black out we hear Orlettas voice

ORLETTA   Ladies and gentlemen before we depart on our world tour I want you to give it up for the Soul Sisters , oh yeah featuring Rufus Collins.

The lights are up and we are at the next nights gig. Orletta walks on and sings lead. We see Rufus enter in a large afro wig. He is one of the backing singers. They break into the Sounds of Blackness Classic

OPTIMISTIC

(SPOKEN)
*NEVER SAY DIE
THE BLACKNESS
NEVER SAY DIE
BE OPTIMISTIC*

The song ends and we have the

Curtain call.

When the crowd have made enough noise they;

Come on again take their places and Orletta sing a fantastic

MIDNIGHT TRAIN TO GEORGIA *by Gladys Knight and the Pips*

As that ends they hit straight into the final song of the night

BOOGIE WONDERLAND *by Earth Wind and Fire.*

*The girls and Rufus **get the audience up onto their feet to dance the rest of the night away. This is gig time.***

The number ends and they leave the stage.

EPILOGUE

As the lights finally go down and the audience think the show is over we hear voiceover of a very excited Maylika. This is a bit like a last scene after the credits of a movie

MAYLIKA   Rufus, Julie, can I introduce you to my friend Peter from EMI. He really wants to talk to you.

We hear the voice of Peter

PETER   Hi, thank you guys, I really enjoyed the show

RUFUS   Thank you.

PETER   I don't know if Maylika told you but I am head of AnR at EMI and I just wanted to know really if you've ever thought about a recording career? Cos if you have I'd love to talk to you about it and see what ideas you might have.

RUFUS   Yeah?

PETER   It would be you and the girls of course

RUFUS   Of course, I wouldn't go any where without Orletta, Pepsi and Maylika.

JULIE   Peter was it? It's funny you should say that, I was only thinking today that what this group needs is an AnR man with the imagination to see that there's more to music than just the teen market. Mature performers are going to be the next big thing. My cuts gone up 25% by the way Rufus....

RUFUS   You're the boss Julie!!!

The band play over the speech.

Lights down

The End.

A collection of the first three plays written by award winning playwright Kwame Kwei-Armah

Bitter Herb
When the eldest son of middle class West Indian **Valerie McKenna** is killed in a racist attack, the ramifications for her and her family are awesome. With each person feeling personally responsible for his death, or blaming the closet one to them, this once seemingly close family being to fall apart at the seams.

Grips with urgency	**The Times**
Mature and provocative theatre	**Daily Express**
A powerful new drama.. echoes of Authur Miller	**Bristol Evening Post**
Important and topical.. a gripping new play	**BBC Radio 3**

Big Nose
Rostands classic love story Cyrano de Bergerac is transported to the Eastern Caribbean and Rackmanque Labroke Grove London Circa 1959, where brilliant calypsonian Clovis Dibiset, rules supreme. However he has to use the aesthetic beauty of Hubert to gain the love of his sweet heart Rosemary.

Hugely impressive.. an adaptation at no odds to the original
Birmingham Post

Fully captures the romance and the comedy
Coventry Evening Telegraph

BBSS/Hold On…
In this searing Soul musical, stuck in the sixties singer Rufus Collins has the bookers coming to see what he thinks will be his 'tribute to the male singing stars of the sixties' show tonight. However what he doesn't know is that his manager has different plans. With out his knowledge or consent she brings his arch enemy Orletta Dupline into his backing vocal line up to 'spice up' the act. However things don't go to plan!

See this! Kwei-Armahs exhilarating feel good musical **The Guardian**
Kwei -Armahs fast moving, soul drenched musical presented here in a new improved, bigger, brighter version-remains an absolute feel good gem .
Venue

ISBN 0-9541226-0-7

RRP £9.99